Richard Barton

Farrago

Containing Essays, moral philosophical, political, and historical : on Shakespeare, truth, etc. - Vol. I

Richard Barton

Farrago

Containing Essays, moral philosophical, political, and historical : on Shakespeare, truth, etc. - Vol. I

ISBN/EAN: 9783337059972

Printed in Europe, USA, Canada, Australia, Japan

Cover: Foto ©ninafisch / pixelio.de

More available books at **www.hansebooks.com**

FARRAGO.

CONTAINING

ESSAYS,

MORAL, PHILOSOPHICAL, PO-
LITICAL, and HISTORICAL:

ON

SHAKESPEARE,	GOVERNMENTS,
TRUTH,	POLITENESS,
BOXING,	ENNUI,
KINGS,	INGRATITUDE,
RELIGION,	FORTUNE,
COMMERCE,	POLITICS, &c. &c.

ABSTRACTS and SELECTIONS on
Various Subjects.

IN TWO VOLUMES.

*Quidquid agunt homines, votum, timor, ira, voluptas
Guadia, difcurfus, noftri eft Farrago libelli.* JUV.

PUBLISHED FOR THE BENEFIT OF THE SOCIETY FOR
THE DISCHARGE AND RELIEF OF PERSONS IM-
PRISONED FOR SMALL DEBTS.

VOL. I.

TEWKESBURY:
Printed and Sold by DYDE and SON.
Sold alfo by P. ELMSLEY in the Strand, and G. and T. WILKIE,
Pater-nofter-row, London.
M,DCC,XCII.

TO THE

SOCIETY

FOR THE

DISCHARGE AND RELIEF

OF PERSONS

IMPRISONED FOR SMALL DEBTS.

GENTLEMEN,

YOUR Inſtitution, viewed in a Political light, is wiſe ; as Humane, is above Praiſe ; Bene quidem dictum eſt, homines maxime Deum imitari, cum beneficia conferunt.

The bleſſings of Lovers, Wives, Parents, and Children, in their frantic joy, when receiving their long-loſt Friends at your hands, are due to your Benevolence.

Permit me to offer my Aſſiſtance, in the Way I think moſt likely to forward the Cauſe you have in hand.

I have the Honour to be,

Gentlemen,

Your moſt obedient Servant,

THE AUTHOR.

THE

CONTENTS

OF THE

FIRST VOLUME.

ESSAYS.

	Page
I. Of Shakefpeare	1
II. — Boxing	9
III. — Friendfhip	15
IV. — Governments	23
V. — Civilized and Savage State	41
VI. — Public Executions	48
VII. — Commerce	57
VIII. — Politics and Politicians	69
IX. — Religion	83
X. — Politenefs	96
XI. — Ennui	101
XII. — Biography	107

XIII.

CONTENTS.

XIII. Of Marriage and Gallantry — 113
XIV. — Truth — — 126
XV. — Kings — — 134
XVI. — Language — 141
XVII. — Ingratitude — 150
XVIII. — Reveries — 156
XIX. — Prudence and Fortune — 169
XX. — Senfibility and Benevolence 181

LETTER on EDUCATION — 194
ENGLISH CONSTITUTION — 219
HISTORY of FRANCE — 235

BLACKSTONE's COMMENTARIES,
OF THE LAWS OF ENGLAND.

Cuftoms — — 269
Countries fubject to the Laws — 277
Rights of Perfons — — 282
The Parliament — — 288
The King and his Title — 293
————'s Prerogative — 297
————Revenue — 306
Revenue Extraordinary — 322
Subordinate Magiftrates — 324
The People — — 337
The Clergy — — 340
The Civil State — 350

The

CONTENTS.

The Military and Maritime	355
Mafter and Servant	360
Hufband and Wife	363
Parent and Child	366
Guardian and Ward	369
Corporations	371
Law of Defcents	375
VICISSITUDES OF OUR GLOBE.	380

ERRATA.

Page 2, r. oscuro
 9, motto, r. cruorem
 58, l. 5, dele not
 62, l. 3, r. maxim
 99, l. 13. r. in villages
 178, l. 8, r. Prudence
 209, l. 1, r. interfered
 220, l. 26, r. usurpation
 214, l. 2, r. swallowed up
 ——— l. 18, r. territorial
 229, l. 13, r. eighth
 238, l. 12, r. succeed
 257, l. 6, r. D'Ancre
 272, l. 11, r. possession
 331, l. 17, r. county.
 376, r. laws

ESSAYS.

ESSAY I.

Of SHAKESPEARE.

Spiritus intus alit, totamque infusa per Artus
Mens agitat molem,——
                                    VIRG.
In this choice work, the God himself we find
Mixt with the mass; HE, fill'd the mighty mind.

SO much has been written concerning our favorite author, that if the subject were not inexhauftible, what any one may have to add, might very well be difpenfed with; but there will ever be caufe for the exertion of the moft enlightened mind, when the exalted merit of this more than mortal, is in queftion; an irrefiftable fervour agitates us, the contemplation of his powers urges the mind to

A   find

find a form of words, adequate to the subject and to its own feelings.

If all other books, and the memory of them, were obliterated, his works alone would illumine the underftanding of the nation, his ever-blooming irradiancy, his unexampled fame, will always be in proportion to the capability of the human mind, as that expands, his tranfcendent mode of information will always be found adequate to the filling it, with admiration and delight.

We muft do the juftice to Garrick, of acknowledging that his exhibitions of fome characters, like the chiaro obfcuro of a picture, brought forward many beauties, which would not fo readily have obtained their value in the general notice. It is now more than thirty years that the thermometer of Shakefpeare's glory, which is graduated to the end of time, has been conftantly rifing.

Of the mind of every other author we can allot the true value of his acquirements, and apportion the *quantum meruit* of his genius, by the common ftandard, but here we are at a lofs for a comparifon.

When we fee him within the compafs of a few

few years, an idle libertine in the country, and then furnifhing plays in the capital, and thofe performances fo much above the caft of mind of the audience, which in general was beft pleafed with what we now reject, it ftrikes us with furprize: The giddinefs of youth might naturally enough precede the moft comprehenfive dormant genius; but at a later period, the hiftory of his holding horfes at the play-houfe, with his affiftant blackguard boys, " puzzles the will," and ftifles all analyfis.

It is in genius, in that divine emanation, which in its nature is inexplicable, that we are to feek the means of refolving this problem.

The author fears, that he may not have the good fortune to explain to others, what he himfelf finds no difficulty to underftand; He thinks the *flatus Dei*, the divinity within, might dictate thofe comprehenfive forms of fpeech, which paffed through Shakefpeare's mind, unnoticed, but as relative to his fubject; intirely without that great effect they communicate to others, and that they were not in any fenfe the refult of reflection, labour, and contrivance, like the

A 2 compofition

compofition of other writers, from him thofe wonders fell, as the ripe acorn unheeded by the oak.

To make this more clear, let us defcend fome fteps from Shakefpeare, and in La Fontaine, we have an inftance of this magic. Thus fpeaks La Bruyere who was his contemporary.

" What fhall I fay of a turn for play, can any one define it for me? is it unneceffary to have forefight, art or clevernefs, to play at chefs or ombre? but if not fo, how comes it that fimpletons fhall excel, and fome of refined underftanding fhall not be able to attain a mediocrity only; to whom a peice, or a card in their hands, fhall trouble the fight, and make them lofe countenance?"

" There is fomething, if it can be, yet more incomprehenfible; a man to appearance vulgar—heavy—ftupid, knows not how to fpeak, nor relate any thing that he fees; if he fits down to write, it is the model of good ftory-telling he makes the animals, the trees and ftones to fpeak, every thing that fpeak not: there is nothing but frolic, elegance, nature, and delicacy in his works."*

Every

* Les Charaƈteres de Theophrafte, tom. 2. p. 114.

Every perſon has noted of his acquaintance, that ſomething which mere chance called forth, has ſet a particular perſon in quite a new point of view. A very ſilly man or woman, may write a card to be admired even, and the verieſt clown, ſhall in ſome difficulties attending his employ, direct a meaſure that Archimedes would have been proud of. Every perſon has a portion of genius, though that portion is oftentimes buried with them; like the ſpark in the flint, it lies hid, unleſs the colliſion of ſomething fitted for the purpoſe, ſhall call forth it's fire.

A RHAPSODY.

DOST thou love pictures?—Look here upon this picture—that has ſo dazzled my reaſon's light.——How infinite in faculties! —in apprehenſion how like a God!—of moſt excellent fancy, either for Tragedy or Comedy—I know not which pleaſes me better —He would drown the ſtage with tears— Then! ſuch ſhaping fantaſies, for jeſt and courteſy! the top of admiration.——

If I ſhould anatomize him to thee as he is —his poſſeſſions are ſo huge—there is not
chaſtity

chaſtity enough in language to utter them—
of wondrous virtues! he is a good divine—
a ſcholar and a ſoldier—ſhines brightly as a
king—a judge—a counſellour—and of government, the properties to unfold, as preg-
nant in, as art and practice has enriched any
—and gives to every power, a power, above
their functions, and their offices—never
ſchool'd, yet learned—and for the liberal arts
without a parallel!—Before my God I might
not this believe, without the ſenſible and true
avouch of mine own eyes.

 Admiring of his virtues—let me have audience for a word or two of commendation
—Heaven nature charg'd, that one body
ſhould be filled with all the graces—'Tis He!
This is He!—His words are my ſoul's food
—ſcrew'd to my memory—of more value
than ſtamps of gold—He's all my exerciſe,
my mirth, my matter—He makes a July's day
ſhort as December—Cures in my thoughts,
that, ſhould chill my blood—I count my-
ſelf in nothing ſo happy, as in a ſoul remem-
b'ring all his matchleſs graces.——

 But, He's gone!—and my idolatrous fancy
muſt ſanctify his relicks—I do beſeech you,
whither is he gone?—I ſpeak to you, Sir—
you

you are certainly a gentleman—clerk-like experienc'd—I pray you mark me—I will prophefy—He is in heaven—ay, by my life —doubt it not—come deal juftly with me— by your fmiling you feem to fay fo—there's a kind of confeffion in your looks—if you think other, remove your thought.—I never fhall be fatisfied till I behold him—to come into his prefence in the court of heaven.——

I do entreat your patience—by the world I count no fable—this is all true, as it is ftrange—think not I flatter—not I, for this fair ifland—that would difhonour him—I fwear I do not—by each particular ftar in heaven, and all their influences—for what advancement may I hope?—no—let the candied tongue lick abfurd pomp, where thrift may follow.—Far behind his worth come all the praifes that I now beftow—well learned is that tongue that well can him commend— I fpeak not this, that you fhould bear a good opinion of my underftanding—affure you— I am forry that with better judgment, I had not quoted him.

This is not my writing, though I confefs much like the character—all this I fpeak in print—for in print I found it.——And fo, fare you well. OUR

OUR SHAKESPEARE only, has the god-like art,
To rouze each paſſion ſlumbring in the heart;
Can pangs of rage, and jealouſy impoſe,
And then with pity every wound can cloſe;
Make airy nothing ſome ſtrange body fill,
Then hail it tyrant, of the human will;
O'er earth, croſs ſeas, through air, from pole to pole,
Can waft in rapture, all the yielding ſoul;
When e'er the maſter waves his magic wand,
The ſenſe refiſtleſs, owns his dread command.

ESSAY

ESSAY II.

Of BOXING.

*Multa cavo lateri ingeminant et pectore vastos
Dant sonitus, duro crepitant sub vulnere malæ,*
—————————— *Crassumque cruorem
Ore rejectantem, mixtosque in sanguine dentes.*
                                              V.IRG.

Againſt the ribs their rawbon'd fiſts they fling,
Their breaſts and chops with ſtrokes redoubled ring,
Till clotted blood, and teeth the ground pollute,
Belch'd from the victor, and the vanquiſh'd brute.

HOW far it may be neceſſary for the ſubſiſtence of the human ſpecies to ſhed blood, we ſhall not inquire, but in India, where a philoſophical ſearch after the hiſtory of the earlieſt tranſactions of mankind naturally conducts us, we find, that the meekeſt and perhaps the moſt happy people, if left to themſelves, ſubſiſt without ſhedding blood. If in colder regions the climate de-
mands

mands a groſſer food, than ſatisfies nature there, and men were induced to attack the innocent herds of cattle which confidently approached them, we may perhaps have ſet the example to the wild beaſts; if we took the hint from them, we claim however the pre-eminence in ſavage cruelty, ſince they, each in their particular ſpecies, have always preſerved a diſtinguiſhed tenderneſs to their fellows.

If war be really neceſſary, the keeping up a ſanguinary ſpirit, and thirſt after blood, becomes ſound policy; the Romans, whoſe traffic was in carnage, might have thought thus, when they regaled the citizens with the fights of gladiators, and combats between men and beaſts,* for they had to encounter, at different times, the moſt ferocious of the human race.

We ſhall endeavour to ſhow how Boxing came into vogue in the eighteenth century, died away, and in the latter part of it, was revived; and why the Greeks upon political principles, refuſed to encourage gymnaſtics.

* They conſtantly procured great numbers of wild beaſts from Africa for the amuſement of the citizens.

About

About fifty years ago, prince William Auguftus duke of Cumberland, countenanced pugilifts, which brought on the decline of what was called the noble fcience of defence, with the broad fword; for it was at that time cuftomary for prize-fighters, as they were termed, to entertain the public with exhibitions of their art; the heroes paraded the market-places on horfeback in their fhirts, with their heads bare, ornamented with fcars; on the fword arm was tied a ribbon, which might be fancied the favour of fome fair one, and at the fame time fwelled the mufcles of the arm, and gave it a more vigorous appearance; a flight cut or two, that the fpectators might have fome blood for their money, decided the combat.

This country is much indebted to his royal highnefs, for infufing that military fpirit which has fhone with fo much luftre, but whether he really believed it ufeful to encourage Boxing, to rouze the dormant courage of the nation, we cannot fay; but many have been perfuaded, that a cold indifference to the fight of blood and wounds, is of ufe to gentlemen who are not of the Clare-market fraternity.

As wars are now managed between us and our enemies, a little more than negative courage is fufficient; we are fo unacquainted with rancour and malice, that apologies and confolations accompany every defeat of the enemy; and who can fay, but in the progrefs of improvement of the human mind, the more enlightened parts of Europe, may at length affert the prerogatives of our nature, and that kindnefs and humanity may fo far prevail, as to fet us above a comparifon with the prowling Lyon.

It is afferted by Galen and was obferved by Xenophon, that boxing, wreftling, and the other violent exertions of ftrength, were attended with defects in fome parts of the body; the boxers and wreftlers wafted from the haunches downwards, whilft thofe who engaged in running and leaping, wafted from the head to the haunches, and many died in early youth of confumptions. They who threw the difk or quoit, had the carnofity of the arm greatly increafed, and the neck loft its natural flexibility. To fome it may appear that thefe exercifes might be made ufeful if moderately purfued, but it is in the nature of emulation to know no bounds, nor medium; one effort produces a greater, a greater, and the victor and conquered are equally enervated by the means they take to render themselves more robust.

Solon perfuaded the Athenians to allot the recompences beftowed on the athletics for the maintenance of orphans, rather than nourifh thofe who were ufelefs both in peace and war; for according to an expreffion of Euripides, they were the worft foldiers in Greece. Thefe men were drawn from the moft vile populace, and if fome of our boxers may pretend to be of a better caft, it muft be owing to the encouragement from their fuperiors, that they have taken up an employment fo atrocious.

If we did not know fome who are generous and courageous, who through habit and careleffnefs of conduct, attend thefe fights, we fhould pronounce againft the poffibility of fuch virtues inhabiting the bofoms of thofe who can be diverted by feeing two naked men hammering each other, till their faces and bodies are covered with blood and contufions; the pertinacity of the man who is knocked down as faft as he can rife, gives us rather a proof of his bafenefs, than of his courage, and fhould difguft every reafonable man;

man; for he is animated to act this brutal part, from a defire of fatisfying the connoiffeurs, of whom he is to receive the wages of fin.

ESSAY

ESSAY III.

Of FRIENDSHIP.

——————— *Et moriens animam abstulit hosti,*
Tum super exanimem sese projecit amicum
Confossus, placidaque ibi demum morte quiescit.
                                        VIRG.

Robb'd of his friend, and wounded, stabs the foe,
Then clasp't in death, they seek the realms below.

FRIENDSHIP is generally the work of a natural impulse, without premeditation or design; if it is assisted by the *mores confimiles*, it soon becomes an unguarded confidence, reciprocally bestowed, 'till at length it takes the appearance of a religious compact. In some it is a charm that softens all the disagreeable accidents which attend human life; it is a consolation to those, even, whose conduct is in other respects void of all sense of honour, who observe no other compact

compact of society; in those who follow the dictates of innocence, it approaches, in it's effects, to that sovereign balm, which preserves human nature from decay.

Almost all the foundations of friendship laid in early life, are intirely disinterested, which a knowledge of the world, in minds not vulgar, rather strengthens.

Friendships, whose basis is in the exchange of social civilities, are likely to have no longer continuance than whilst the sun shines; a lively agreeable man may have as many of these as he pleases, and if from his frankness of heart he admits a warmer attachment than may belong to others, whilst it lasts, he has the advantage; if any misfortune befalls him and he estimates his friends by his own feelings, he may chance to suffer a disappointment.

> *Donec eris felix multos numerabis amicos,*
> *Tempora si fuerint nebula, solus eris.**

But let us disregard all trite sayings that circumscribe the human mind, it is sometimes found that friendship will ripen and bear fruit

---
* Friends you may have, while pleasure you bestow,
All hate and shun a discontented brow.

early in fome breafts, with very little cultivation.

We believe that there are more good actions fpring from whim and caprice, than from the beft regulated moral conduct. Every body knows, there are more whimfical men than philofophers, but no one knows the motive of generofity in another, nor is it our bufinefs.

A breach of friendfhip is generally accompanied with very atrocious behaviour on one fide; to form a friendfhip there muft always be the appearance of a more than common kindnefs, to engage another in a like predilection for ourfelves; to cover the levity and injuftice of finifhing this commerce, the traitor generally begins by calumniating his friend, relying on the partiality of that bofom, wherein he lodged his poifon; and in this he does, what he often dares not do even to a perfon who has offended him.

Cæfar repelled all the affaffins as they advanced, till he faw Brutus, he then wrapped his face in his garment, and bowed his head; the friend, and not the poniard, terrified the hero.

The duke de Rochefaucault, first broached this false maxim, "In the adversity of our friends we always find something that does not displease us." Dean Swift, who was a disappointed man, humoursome and petulant, seems to exult in this discovery. In the best palliation of it, in the desire to give assistance to our friend, the motive is unfriendly, and unwise, although not quite shameful.

Lucretius was a better moralist:

Suave mari magno turbantibus æquora ventis
E terra magnum alterius spectare laborem,
Non quia vexari quemquam est jucunda voluptas,
Sed quibus ipse malis careas, quia cernere suave est.

From land if pleased, while some the billows brave,
We view them struggling 'gainst a wat'ry grave,
In the disaster we no pleasure find,
Our safety, not their danger, cheers the mind.

If this unkindness were a natural defect, we should have much more to deplore in our constitutional make, but as we know an instance to the contrary, we presume there are many who never found such a thought floating in the mind, even for a moment; but where that may be the first impression, if it is subdued immediately, like many other mental suggestions against a strict moral conduct,

duct, in the ftate of our probation here, the refiftance makes a part of what we make no fcruple to call, a pious difcharge of our duty. A good man may be tempted to appropriate to himfelf a fum of money intrufted to him, where no means of detection can follow; but if he refifts it, there would no ftain remain on his character, if he were publickly to own that he had been fo affailed. A never-failing fpontaneous defire to do good, is above our nature.

Rochefaucault fays too, " That what we call friendfhip, is only a reciprocal management of intereft, and an exchange of good offices; a commerce where felf-love always expects to gain fomething,"—" That you fhould love fo, as you may one day hate,"— " That, it is a proof of little friendfhip, not to perceive the coolnefs of a friend," and yet he fays in another place, " That it is more fhameful to fufpect a friend, than to be deceived by him;" and in twenty-fix maxims on this fubject, there is like want of confiftency.

Lord Chefterfield has recommended Rochefaucault's Thoughts and Maxims, of which we think," that notwithftanding it has enjoyed a great reputation, it is sometimes unintelligible ; it contains many truths of an old date, with some reflections that are just and sensible ; many things disgusting, which represent man as an incorrigible beast; and very few maxims that are useful and improving."

Let us hear honest Montaigne, who suffered the inward man to go his course, without curbing him, in order to show his own ingenuity : " What I call friendship," says he, " is indivisible, each gives himself so intirely to the other, that there remains nothing that can be self-appropriated. He is vexed that he has not two or three souls, all interested the same way with his single one ; it is a miraculous way of doubling one's self, or one soul in two bodies; there is no giving or lending ; if there is a distinction, the receiver confers the favour; if I wanted any thing of my friend, I should send to redemand it, as if he had formerly received it of me."

This we confess is an enthusiasm that is not, that cannot burn, in every breast, but there are many degrees of friendship between this, and the meanness of Rochefaucault's blessed bleffed commerce; but it muft be the fate of every thing that is governed by the difpofitions and reafonings of mortal men, to be fubject to an infinity of defcriptions; fo that general definitions prove only the vanity of thofe, who attempt to circumfcribe the human mind by a kind of oracular decifion. As the neceffity of loving one another is fo evident, it is wonderful that a pleafure fhould be found in propagating things, that tend to difunite, and make us odious to each other; and, that perfons in other refpects of good underftanding, fhould fo readily adopt them.

There is nothing has fuch influence on the human mind as the voice of a friend; we know he ftudies our own intereft; he may make a miftake, but he will not deceive us: The unfortunate man who is without a friend, is doubly miferable if he has fenfibility; for though his friend may not have the power to take the load from his fhoulders, the contemplation of his fincere defire to do it, is a great confolation.

A man often wants more force than his own to fupprefs fome defires that might prove injurious to him; the advice of a friend is the only check on fuch an occafion, he fees

the

the things in a clear point of view, whilst the other is blinded by passion or folly.

In the tender love between the sexes, if in a due course of time the attachment changes to a warm friendship, it is the triumph of unequivocal virtue.

ESSAY

ESSAY IV.

Of GOVERNMENTS.

——Pauci reges, non regna colunt.

SEN.

How few who wait obsequious round a throne,
The country's welfare seek, and not their own!

THE nature and origin of different Governments have employed the reflection and ingenuity of many writers, the greater part of whom have adopted a systematic reasoning, to dress up a theory that should meet the particular kind of Government of which they were treating, rather than trace it through the changes and chances it had undergone, before it assumed the character it is known by; in doing which they abandon the harder task, they frame arguments from what they see effected, and call their deductions from them, the principles of this or that government.

The great Montesquieu has shown us what he deems to be the principles of the republican, monarchical, and despotic, Governments, but he left us to find out that there is none of those respective Governments at this time, nor ever were, which grew out of those principles, or did ever subsist by them.

Governments are subject to mutability equally with every other thing in the world, however gradual and imperceptible in their changes, when compared with those things, which are more particularly the object of our senses. Our own, which is well defined for the most part by a system of positive law, is however different, in many instances, from what it was in the reigns of George the first and second; and within these last thirty years it has undergone very visible changes: The same may be said of every Government in Europe.

They who trace the origin of Government from domestic subordination, indulge in the luxuriance of fancy; it may hold good thus far,

far, that the coalition of members of all Governments were at firſt of ſmall numbers, who had experience of no other ſubjection, than that which is natural or domeſtic ; but the principles that are the life of domeſtic happineſs, though they may influence the mind of a good magiſtrate in a ſmall degree, are unfit for his general application ; the functions of a father of a family are eaſily diſtinguiſhed from the fundamental and neceſſary laws of ſociety. The voice of nature is the beſt counſellor to a good father, but would be a falſe guide to the magiſtrate, who muſt follow no other rule than the public reaſon, or the law ; it is not, therefore, difficult to find good fathers, but to find men fit to govern others, is no eaſy taſk, as we may learn from hiſtory.

It ſeems at firſt ſight no groſs preſumption to point out eſſential improvements in the beſt Government, and to carry them ſo far, as to exclude all the ſources of injuſtice and diſcord, and to embrace every thing ſalutary; but we have lately ſeen how difficult it is to arrange the combination of qualities ſo heterogenous, as are involved in a machine ſo very complex. The American States, who have the advantage of ſo many models, may be esteemed very fortunate, if they put any thing together, that will keep out the weather for a long time; and the French may teach us, how many inconveniences attend very material alterations in a fixed form of Government; insomuch that we may deem it impossible to be effected, but in a long course of time and experience.

The Americans are likely to succeed sooner than the French, because of the greater division of landed property. It is difficult to give a poor man true ideas of liberty; he understands it only as it is contra-distinguished to confinement.

Concerning the causes of the French Revolution, it may be observed, that for fifty years past, the Government had been more oppressive than any in Europe, if the nature of its constitution, and the spirit of the people, be considered; a determination to love their prince, seems to have been the magic that kept every thing in its place.

The last years of Louis the fifteenth, were so profligately disrespectful to his subjects, that it was wonderful there was no revolt; the whole nation was sensible of their situation,

tion, the language of the parliaments was intelligible to the meaneſt capacity, and filled every mind ; it was the language of the an‑cient republicans, and at the expence of the fortunes and liberties of the patriots who uſed it, in their remonſtrances to the prince. Let any one reflect that no miniſter had dared to refuſe the payment of thoſe enormous ſums, drawn for by Madame du Barri, and her minions ; for this irregularity in the treaſury was not limited to herſelf.

It is ſaid, that among the papers of the late king of Pruſſia, was found one, which, in a manner, predicted the event which has happened, from the publication of certain philoſophical or atheiſtical writings of Diderot, D'Alembert, and ſome others ; Mr. Burke makes this alſo the chief cauſe of the revolution ; impoſing as ſuch authority may appear, we ſhall venture another opinion.

It may be allowed that an emancipation from the enthuſiaſm of a religion not reaſo‑nable, may ſtrengthen the mind, and fit it for bolder diſcuſſions, than it would have otherwiſe engaged in ; but we believe the increaſe of taxes from the American war, and the very reprehenſible conduct near the

throne

throne, had more influence on this occaſion.

Is it difficult to believe that a wounded ſoldier in an hoſpital in America, ſhould reflect, that he had been ſhedding his blood to ſecure liberty to a people, who were oppoſing their ſovereign; a people, whom, a few months before, he had confidered as the enemies of his country, and that he was to return home, to a nation, which had not the ſpirit to reſent the injuries they complained of? Is it a miracle that an army with theſe notions, ſhould infect the whole maſs of people when they got home, and furniſh the means of their deliverance? Is it a wonder that the fiſh-women at Paris ſhould make more converts to ſuch a cauſe, than the abſtruſe reaſoning on ſubjects incomprehenſible, in language, baſe and vulgar, as Mr. Burke calls the profane writings of the philoſophical atheiſts?

Theſe arguments lie upon the ſurface we confeſs, and may therefore be rejected by politicians, who prefer things hidden from ordinary reaſonable men.

The Czar Peter changed ſome of his Ruſſian

fian fubjects into the appearance of Germans, but the lateft accounts inform us that the effects upon the whole empire were not very confiderable, and there is perhaps an equal chance of its going back in another century to its former uncivilized manners; as to its advancement to a comparifon with the moft polifhed countries in Europe: In a defpotic ftate every thing depends on the prince.

We know that there muft be changes in the nature of all things which are the objects of the laws; of courfe the laws ought to be accommodated to the changes: Religion, commerce, manners, riches, increafe of territory, or lofs of a part, and an innumerable detail of circumftances, make it neceffary that their influence fhould be attended to; how many ftatutes are now obfolete and unrepealed, that originally were framed in wifdom? but innovations are neverthelefs dangerous, when there is a chance of their affecting any of the great wheels of the political machine; it is better to fit down under an evil, the extent of which is known, than to rifk an encounter with what may prove a greater; for fome inconvenience will attend every thing of human conftruction.

The

The inquiry concerning the origin of nations, is fo encumbered with uncertainty, as to render it as diffatisfactory as the fearch after the firft fettlement of the elephants; and that of the different Governments is no lefs perplexed. The firft inftitutes of whatever nature they might be, were impofed by the force of mind and body of one, or a coalition with as many as were neceffary to compel the reft; and in what other manner is order maintained at this time, however difguifed in different countries, with appearances favorable to the difpofitions and cuftoms of the people? The ideas concerning what is natural, and muft, therefore, have been employed in the firft forming any Government, and the jargon of firft principles applied to things wholly fortuitous, is ridiculous.

It is an idle theory to pretend that a people emerging from a favage ftate, fhould fall into a regular provifion againft evils they had never experienced, and which were to grow out of their herding together; they were doubtlefs firft inftructed by fome inconveniences becoming intolerable, before they thought of rectifying them; the next thing they learned, was to fubmit with patience

to

to such evils as a superior force refused to remedy.

We see something of the parcelling out conquests in the feudal system of our ancestors, and that most of the Governments of Europe rose from that; but concerning the institution of the feudal compact, who can inform us? we may conclude that it grew out of envy, malice, discord, and throat-cutting; and we know that it died away by the exertion of the same violences, directed to another point.

We insist that no Government was ever framed, where the happiness of the people was the first consideration; though most system-mongers pretend, that, this is the nature of things, is a first principle in the formation and coalition of small numbers, to complete what we call a nation; if we are right, it could not exist at an early period, and if it does not exist now in any state, let them show when it did. There are some Governments where the happiness of the people is never thought of, and many, where the people are considered only as relative to the permanence of the state, as mortar in the composition of a wall; and yet perhaps there is no abfurdity in faying, that notwithftanding the known abfence of good intentions in thofe who govern, the people of all countries, generally fpeaking, prefer their own governments to others.

One may affert of thofe patriots the moft active in effecting the revolution, that their firft idea of it fprung from the inconveniences attending their own particular fortunes and circumftances; that it carried with it a favour to the people they could eafily fee, and this could be no objection, as they muft be the means to bring it about; but that the incitement was the interefts and happinefs of the people, no one who is acquainted with the difpofitions of thofe who are bufied in politics, can ever believe. This is not meant to leffen the merits of thofe who took the lead, for it would be ungrateful to deny that the public received great benefits, and that thofe benefits could not have accrued without the interference of the moft active.

Some Englifh writers intoxicated with the charms of our prefent government, have affected to fpeak of it, as a natural right and inheritance, and have infifted that the principles of it, have at all times exifted againft
the

the fulleſt evidence of ſeveral inſtances at different periods, when the moſt ſtupid ſervility in all ranks prevailed in England, more than in France; we may take the reign of Henry the Eighth for one, at which time, and for many ages before, there perhaps never had been a ſingle man in Europe, capable of entertaining complete ideas of the nature and benefits of ſuch laws, as our conſtitution is compoſed of; we allow that all mankind have a natural right to freedom, and to exact from their governors ſuch things as they think conducive to their happineſs; but to argue that this was an excluſive right inherent in the conſtitution of this country, is ridiculous.

The ſtruggles of the nobility for leſſening the power of the reigning princes, prove nothing relative to general freedom; to every one endowed with a capacity to diſtinguiſh the eſſential parts of a good Government, there is nothing more clear, than that we now live under, is ſo much above every other inſtitution, that ever did exiſt, in all the great qualities that conſtitute freedom, and ſafety of perſon and property, that no era in the long detail of hiſtory, can furniſh any thing to be put in compariſon with it;

but let no man attribute this felicity to human foresight and contrivance. There was a time when the people of France stood fairer to emancipate themselves than we did; the king of England copied the French king in granting privileges to the burghers, to enable them to oppose the nobility; this was the first step to our general freedom, though by no means intended to introduce the consequences; in the round of vicissitudes we have attained what the French at that time did not acquire, and we ought to acknowledge that those who found it, were in search of they knew not what; we owe our glorious situation to the pertinacity of a deluded and deluding hot-brained enthusiasm, and not to the quiet fervour of philosophy and good sense.

It is easy to suppose that the lower orders of people in some countries in Europe, may prefer the Government under which they have been brought up, to that we make our boast of; accustomed from their first acquaintance with life, to a slavish obedience to their superiors, they know of nothing more natural, and so long as they feel not the scourge of injustice, they have no cause of discontent.

The

The pride attending power and pre-eminence in the nobility of those countries, is alike natural; they think it very reasonable that they should be esteemed of more value than the common people, of whose origin from the dust of the earth, they have a ready conception; it is not in the nature of man to be disgusted with undisturbed favour and distinction. There are some gentlemen here, not quite contented with the small distinction, as they think it, between themselves and their inferiors: The blackguard is as apt to over-rate the majesty of his person and prerogatives, as the gentleman may be; and, in a violent dispute for preference, if the gentleman cannot show, by a syllogism drawn from bone and muscles, that he too is sprung from earth, he must submit, and reckon his temporary degradation amongst the taxes he pays for being a gentleman.

We justly admire our ancient institution of trials by juries, as the most likely means to come at an impartial decision; it bears, however, the marks of human imperfection, owing perhaps, in some measure, to the time of its birth, when there were only two sorts of people in the kingdom, the nobility and commonalty.

commonalty. There are many cafes where the common run of jurymen are incompetent judges, of what may nearly affect a man's honour and his life; it would be very difficult to provide against it, but the fairnefs in the proceedings in our courts, makes it indeed almoft unneceffary.

The Canadians fince they fell under our dominion, preferred the fummary mode of military law, to trials by jury; and amongft that rank too, we fhould be apt to conclude, ftood moft in need of protection: but there is a fallacy in judging of others from our own feelings. Thofe who have never feen an inftance where it was the duty of a fuperior to liften to their complaints, and whom they could compel to render them juftice, have fo debafed an opinion of themfelves, that they are incapable of conceiving any thing like our laws. Suppofe our Government offered to the Turks, it is likely it might appear fo repugnant to their ideas, as to be rejected; to fay nothing of its coming from infidel dogs: a man muft here take a great deal of pains before he can get his head taken off, and there he has the felicity of not knowing to whom it may belong to-morrow; and

and this, in the extravagancies of the human mind, may be reckoned for something: it is certain, that the pachas and other officers, who partake of power, accept it on terms that would never perfuade us; and, therefore, the precarious tenure by which a man holds his head, may have fweets, of which we cannot judge, and perhaps may be confidered by them, with the indifference, that the diftinction between free and copyhold is with us: if it were the cuftom here, for my lord duke to be regaled now and then with the baftinado, no private gentleman, in like circumftances, would confider himfelf ruined in fame and fortune.

Spain is a defpotic Government, but fo tempered by the influence of the clergy, and fome cuftoms, that there is no country where pride, and loftinefs of felf-conceit, prevail more, among the common people: we may pretend to vie with her, but the fame whims do not with us produce fo much content and good order: the ferene blue fky of Spain fofters complacency and good humour; a drunken blackguard, a wretch loft to all fenfe of dignity, is unknown there.

However highly we may eftimate our liberty,

berty, which it is to be hoped will never sink in its value, there has been an instance in Europe, and in a people not a little allied to us in blood, where it was thought not worth preserving; the commons, enraged at some pretensions of the nobility to be excused taxation, made a present of their rights of every kind, to the king, who, from being elective and of very confined powers, became immediately absolute, and his crown hereditary, and so continues; this happened in Denmark, in 1660, soon after this country had gone into the most violent measures to gain that right, which the others held of such small account: if the Danes are at present in a contented state, we may assert, that there cannot be any thing more delusive than the comparative state of content in one country, taken from that, which may be the basis of it in another.

Let us consider the lowest and most forlorn state in which a man can be born, that of being a slave to the lord of the soil, where he is native; it appears at first view difficult to allot any consolation to such a situation, but let us not be in haste to set bounds to human ingenuity; the difference there is between one master and another must be allowed

to

GOVERNMENTS.

to have a wide range, in which many flattering circumstances may be involved; one lord may be an inhuman brute, but another may be a tender guardian through life; but taking the worst, which is not likely to be confined to a single instance in such a forlorn situation, a man may perhaps have a pride in belonging to an estate of a larger extent or of a better soil than some others, or that in his master's family are reckoned a greater number of princes; and possibly most of our pleasures, if severely scrutinized, may be found to arise from impositions on ourselves, no less gross.

What we call liberty, and the want of it, may in different circumstances, be of less consequence in diffusing national content than we are aware of; to suppress a little our vaunting disposition, concerning the happy state of our political arrangement, it may not be amiss to recollect that faction, venality, and corruption, produce not the firmest foundation, on which the happiness of a people may be placed.

Montesquieu, after describing the English constitution, concludes thus: " As all human things have a termination, the state of which

we

we have been speaking will lose its liberty, and will perish; Rome, Sparta and Carthage have sunk; it will perish when the Legislative Power shall be more corrupt than the Executive." This is one of his political parables; by the side of which we shall place a ridiculous story: A raree-show-man was exhibiting the court of France to some boys; There, says he, you see the Court of France —there you see the King of France—and the Dauphin of France.——The lad at the glass cries out——which is the King of France? ——which is the Dauphin of France?—— The answer was, which you please my little master, which you please.

Ridentem dicere verum,
Quid vetat? *

---

* Nice ears might tingle should plain truth be spoke,
  Humour the failing, tell it as a joke.

ESSAY

ESSAY V.

Of the CIVILIZED AND SAVAGE STATE.

*Omnibus una quies, venter senfufque per artus,
Ingeniumque capax, varias educit in artes.*
MANIL.

All feek for eafe, for fenfual joys and food,
By various arts acquire, what each thinks good.

WHETHER the animal man is more happy in the Civilized or Savage State, is a queftion that has been often agitated under thofe prejudices, which it were vain to hope fhould be feparated from it: the mind of the moft acute metaphyfician is precifely as incapable of fixing the juft value on the comforts attending the Savage Life, for comforts there are, as the favage man is from estimating the charms which chain us down to Civil Society.

There is good reason to believe, that the savage is the more contented being; a ship, a watch, fine buildings, or whatever may be shown to him as efforts of ingenuity, awaken no curiosity in him; to say that he despises them as unworthy his notice, is more than we know; but it is certain that he betrays none of that admiration and anxiety about them, which can give us cause to believe that he wishes to possess the power of acquiring such things.

It may be suspected, that our notions of superiority are supported by an over-weening pride in us, and not by a firm and settled opinion of our advantages. Curiosity and inquisitiveness arise from doubt and uneasiness, from which the savage is free; the things we have mentioned to be rated high in our esteem are to him as a blank or void; he resembles the child, who was carried to St. Paul's church for the purpose of observing the effect it would have upon him; he said nothing of the stupendous building, but a box, built for the watchman, caught his eye, as a proper house for a large dog that was at home. The

The favage has no defire to migrate, that he may partake of our benefits, but we are envious of many things which he poffeffes, whilft we face every danger and toil to become acquainted with them ; the plea of commercial views ferves to glofs over the confeffion of our wants, but it alfo fhows that we are not contented with what we already have; if therefore the difpute is, which is the moft contented in his ftation, it muft be given againft us.

To fay, that we ought to be more fatisfied than the favage, is mere declamation; the affiftance we derive from the aggregate of our ingenuity in fociety, to whatever it is applied, is always attended with a countervailing fomething of evil ; fo that in an exact ratio, the higher we carry our improvements to gratify our fenfes, the more we increafe our inability to enjoy them : to fome, the hope of procuring them is denied ; whilft thofe on whom they are beftowed, are from the facility of gratification, too faftidious to be pleafed with them ; which is the reafon that thofe perfons are efteemed the wifeft amongft us, who have brought themfelves to have the feweft wants, or in other words, who in this sense, approach the nearest to the state of the savage, or man contented with what he has.

Rousseau, who from extreme sensibility, was incapable of properly sustaining the trifling incidents belonging to social intercourse, was inclined to prefer the pleasures arising from solitude; but how does the solitude of a disgusted brain-sick man apply to that of one in savage life, who is without care, but to satisfy his animal wants, and without reflection, but how to employ his bodily force to acquire them?

Dr. Johnson, whose only enjoyment was in society, would have made no hesitation in deciding against the gross absurdity of comparing the two states; he would have called the under-valuing our powers of improvement a dereliction of the best quality of our nature; the content arising from idleness, and exemption from reflection, he would have branded with the title of the same atrocious perversion of God's benefits, which justly condemned the fallen angels to their state of misery.

If we suppose a man to be taken from savage

vage life, and to become civilized, the argument will be in no better ftate from his opinion; he would have exchanged one fet of habits and prejudices for another, that's all. Omai had a tolerably fair trial of the difference between the two ftates, but he has given us no reafon to conclude that what he found amongft us created any difguft in him to return to his former way of life; in Captain Cook's opinion, his acquirements of every kind would be more than counterbalanced by the evils that would attend them.

It was obfervable on the peace in 1763, after the Indian war carried on in North America by Colonel Bouquet, that amongft the Indians were fome young men, who had been made prifoners at a time of life capable of diftinguifhing between things needful and comfortable, and the want of them; who from a few years cohabitation with the Indians returned to their parents arms with every expreffion of forrow and diftrefs at parting with favage life, feeming to prefer the happinefs of their relations to their own in the conflict; and it was not doubted, that if their parents had not been prefent to receive them, they would not have quitted
their

their laſt connections, to have returned to their former; it requires ſome pertinacity to refuſe to admit theſe facts as an argument, if not deciſive, to be, however, of very great weight in favour of ſavage life.

He that ſuffers the leaſt miſery is the moſt happy, and he the moſt miſerable who feels the feweſt pleaſures: this is a diſtinction common to both the ſituations we are ſpeaking of, and deſcriptive of our negative ſtate of happineſs in this world, which muſt be meaſured by the leaſt quantity of evils ſuffered, to determine the preference: the uncultivated mind, or man in his natural ſtate as it is called, has clearly the advantage; as moſt of our uneaſineſſes are derived from reflection, which is the effect of an increaſe of our ideas and ſenſibility.

The real world has its bounds, the imaginary one is infinite, which is a kind of epitome of the human mind in its naked and cultivated ſtate. To place the queſtion in half the points of view only, that might be found appoſite, would carry us much beyond our preſent purpoſe, we ſhall therefore diſmiſs it with this aſſertion, which appears to be the true ſtate of the caſe: That we are

all

CIVILIZED AND SAVAGE STATE 47

all the children of habit, that man is doomed by his nature in every condition, to carry a burden equal to his ſtrength; the changes of ſituation, various as they are, from the ſavage to the higheſt perfection of civil life, are but a kind of ſhifting the load; ſo that the forlorn, unſophiſticated inhabitant of Terra del Fuego may be ſuppoſed to enjoy as large a portion of content, as the moſt accompliſhed courtier, in the moſt brilliant drawing-room in Europe.

ESSAY

ESSAY VI.

Of

PUBLIC EXECUTIONS.

THE public executions in this country have rather a tendency to harden such of the spectators as are embarked in vicious courses, by holding out flattering examples to them, in favour of their general maxim, " a short life and a merry one," which they oppose to the dull prospect of procuring a maintenance, by strenuous honest labour.

There is no observation more common, than that of the condemned convicts dying well, or as the vulgar term it, " like a cock;" this often proceeds from a cause directly contrary to that which is assigned, namely, courage.

PUBLIC EXECUTIONS.

courage. An excefs of timidity to meet death, will make a man grieve till nature is exhaufted of her tears, a placid refignation follows, which is fupported by the view of his inevitable fate; befides which, the hopes of a remiffion of future mifery, through the mercies held out by religion, take place in fome, and in others, vanity, the laft vital fpark that quits the human frame, animates, even the moft atrocious, to make a momentary difplay of fomething generally admired and excites them to be emulous of that fame, which has been beftowed on others in like circumftances.

The influence of punifhments, on the fpectators, is regulated by what they fee, and whatever may be the extent of that, if it is nicely proportioned to the crime, which is not always eafy to fix, will excite the neceffary terrour, whether it be the halter, the rack, or the refinements of tyrannic cruelty.

If inftead of a public exhibition of fuch as the law had doomed to fuffer its extreme feverity, an act of parliament were paffed, for conducting the punifhment privately in the prefs-yard, and upon fome occafions, that the corpfe fhould be expofed on a ftage erected

ted for that purpofe, before the prifon, it might tend to fix that terrour in the minds of the common people, which is the object of the Legiflative; the fight of the lifelefs lump, would raife many ideas in the fpectators, concerning the fuffrings of the fubject of their curiofity; they would fuppofe cruelties in the executioner which had not been practifed, fuch as the refufal of his affiftance to fhorten the pains of the punifhment, a denial of only one minute more of exiftence, and a variety of other circumftances, would croud upon their minds, of a melancholy caft; whereas in our public executions, which are fo frequent, the feries is fo conftantly uniform, and the fentence executed with fo much tendernefs, that the fear of death in that fhape is ftifled in all thofe who by their difhoneft habits, are forced into the confideration, that their career will finifh with a like cataftrophe.

The objects of punifhments being to deter, or prevent the criminal from doing the fame in future, and to excite an abhorrence of his crime and infamy in others, that which is beft proportioned to the nature of the deed, will make the moft efficacious and durable
impreffion

impreffion on all; in this country, the legal punifhments are always inflicted, fo as to convey the idea of lenient juftice, and the total abfence of paffion and tyranny.

The pains impofed on Damiens, as a punifhment for his attack on the life of Louis XV, were cruel and unjuft, for if the caufe be traced to its fource, it will be found to have taken its rife in the folly and vice of the religion of the country; to the truth of which, the expulfion of the jefuits, fince, bears teftimony; and indeed it may be afferted, that an act fo atrocious as the affaffination of a king, between whom, and his fubject there are fo many intervening caufes to fhield him from perfonal malice, can fcarcely ever happen but from madnefs, or the beaftly fury of fanaticifm.

Excefs of punifhments not only ftrains the minds of the fufferer to meet the ferocity of the law, but it is a fpur to the commiffion of many crimes, to avoid the penalty, which would be inflicted on one only; for which reafon it is, that in thofe countries where the law is exceffive in feverity, the hand of the legiflator may be faid to guide that of the affaffin; if a man is to be tortured for a highway robbery, he will commit a murder to prevent a difcovery.

What mode of punifhment is there which does not debafe the dignity of human nature? it is painful to a generous mind to look upon the trifling punifhment, as it is thought, of whipping; how repugnant then to the philantrophy cherifhed in fuch a breaft, is the idea of deliberately inflicting death? how difmal to reflect that the misfortune of his fellow creature originated in the neglect of thofe whofe duty it was to have put him in the right way, and who perhaps perverted his mind at a time it was equally difpofed to have received wholfome inftruction! whilft others urge the neceffity of punifhments, the philofopher in filence laments, that more care is not taken by the legiflature, to prevent fuch calamities.

If it be hopelefs to think of effecting in a fhort time, the means of preventing thofe evils which difturb the repofe and fafety of fociety, it is not fo with refpect to the remedy for preventing the predetermined murders, that are fo frequently made the morning amufement of many thoufands.

The

The safe-guard to the welfare of the common people is a spirit of induſtry, all incitements to honeſt labour, carry with them ſure means of content, and in proportion as the wiſdom of the legiſlature is exerted to attain that point, a nation is well or ill governed; many of our laws have this object in view, but a variety of accidents remote from our preſent purpoſe to deſcribe, has rendered the political ſyſtem of government in this country, and the happineſs of the people, diſtinct objects; in ſome caſes, they are at open war with each other, we find therefore the leſs to wonder at, if the conſequences ſhould fall heavy upon the lower orders of ſociety.

It is unneceſſary to enumerate the cauſes which have brought about a defection of manners, and of the morals of the common people; a concurrence of circumſtances which always accompany the purſuit of an encreaſe of commerce and riches, has had the ſame effects here, which it has had at all times and in all places, wherever it ſpreads its baneful influence; inſomuch that it may be deemed an axiom, that the greateſt commercial people is in danger of becoming the moſt ſcoundrel nation.

We

We are positive that the welfare of the lower people is attached to their habits of industry, for almost every species of wickedness which calls for the rigorous arm of the magistrate, arises from the desertion of those principles, which are known to the meanest capacity; and if we are certain that a man commits a robbery, because he will not work, we have the proper punishment before our eyes.

When a man is certain that if he is convicted of a robbery he shall be sentenced to labour the remainder of his life in durance, under an unrelenting taskmaster, it may be supposed that he will rather settle his inclination to maintain himself by an unrestrained regulation of labour, than run the risk of the constantly irksome punishment attending that temporary relaxation from work, which theft or any other unlawful measure may furnish.

Should this kind of punishment be adopted, it might check that depravity of character, which is no rarity in the metropolis, that of having decidedly given the preference in favour of idleness, followed by an ignominious death, when even it might happen, rather than

than to exift on a more fcanty allowance, refulting from honeft labour.

Places might be contrived at Plymouth,
Portfmouth, and all the great arfenals, where
thefe people fhould be employed to fome national benefit, in return for their depredations on the public: a plan very different
from the practice in our prifons muft be
followed, no perfon fhould be fuffered to
fee them, or hear of them, till their behaviour had obtained fo much favour from
their governors, who, upon a proper amend-
ment in them, might be allowed to recommend them as proper to make a part of the
civil community; the habits of daily labour, and the hopes of enlargement, would
undoubtedly produce a reformation in moft
of them. Some have pretended that the
fight of flaves, as they term thefe people,
might in time beget a want of refpect for
liberty, in the nation; our plan precludes the
appearance of thefe men out of their proper
place: but we think that the frequent fight
of them in the ftreets, if requifite, could not
produce any uncomfortable ideas, when they
were confidered, as men making retribution
to the public, and in the road to reformation

and

and future happiness; whereas the Homicides we have mentioned, might disgust a Catabaw Indian; the odium and expence, of sending so many of our countrymen to the uttermost parts of the earth, rather than take the pains to make them useful and happy subjects, might be avoided. It is at least our duty, if we are more enlightened than our forefathers, to do all we can, that we may have no cause to exclaim———

> *Ætas parentum pejor avis tulit*
> *Nos nequiores, mox daturos*
> *Progeniem vitiosiorem.**
>
> HOR.

---

* From age to age Vice takes a wider course,
Bad as we are, our sons will yet be worse.

ESSAY

ESSAY VII.

Of COMMERCE, *and its* EFFECTS.

———*Lucri bonus est odor, ex re*
Qualibet———————
Unde habeas quærit nemo, sed oportet habere.
                                                    JUVENAL.

Through hands unhallowed should your profit pass,
Greet it with welcome, think it no disgrace;
Take care to get enough, and none will blame,
Nor over curious, ask from whence it came.

THE benefits of Commerce are so manifold and obvious, that argument is unnecessary to recommend it as an object of national concern, of the greatest consequence; if we consider it however in a philosophical light, we shall discover some things belonging to it, which are generally passed
over

over by those who have written on the subject, with the design only of setting forth its advantages; the progress it has made in this country within the last forty years has exceeded all expectation; but as it was not not only out of sight and calculation of human reach, and in many instances in opposition to it, we must allow that it has arisen out of accidents; and though it should be probable that it may yet extend itself so as to produce still greater riches, it must at all times be subject to a variety of circumstances, some of which may be of such baneful influence, as to cause the most calamitous species of ruin.

Industry is productive of happiness to mankind in whatever manner it is applied; it is an inexhaustible spring of profit and delight; it is a quality so beneficial, that a person who by reflection, or habit, is master of this turn of mind, is in a manner endowed with a sixth sense; the power and force of a nation may be multiplied to any degree to which this spirit can be exerted, whether it is called forth into action in war or peace; without it every thing is languid and unprosperous.

Almost

Almoſt all the moral and phyſical evils of human life grow out of idleneſs, and as it is the nature of man to require compulſion to bring his active powers into uſe, it ſhould be the principal care of every well-regulated community to encourage a propenſity to labour, and to plant in the members of it, a more vigorous activity of mind than nature has beſtowed; and this cannot ſo generally be effected, as by employing the labour of the people, in exchange for that of other nations, through the medium of Commerce.

Thoſe philoſophers, who inſiſt that nature has been too ſparing of that quality of the mind which ſhould induce us to reliſh labour, muſt, however, allow that ſhe does not refuſe the reward for the attainment of it; the cheerfulneſs of temper which accompanies a truly induſtrious occupation, produces ſenſations which indolence can never furniſh, even with the aſſiſtance of riches; there is no ſtate of mankind totally exempt from the neceſſity of ſometimes exerting a vigorous application of the body and mind, and all are equally ſenſible of its advantages;

*Æque pauperibus prodeſt, locupletibus æque.**

* The poor and rich alike their profit find.

It is by the national spirit of industry that the weight of our enormous debt is not only made tolerable, but useful; for its magnitude is only a greater spur, so long as it exceeds not some certain limits. Let us suppose a man to work constantly half the day on account of the public, and the rest for the maintenance of himself and family; we shall find him in a happier situation than if he had completed his own business in half the time, and given no assistance to the public: those artisans employed in manufactures which yeild the highest price to the labourer, and are under the necessity of working only three days in the week, bestow the rest of the time, generally speaking, in dissipation, or in other words, in doing that they should not do, and contract habits productive of poverty, and of discontent, which is a greater evil: a course of constant labour, to furnish what is absolutely necessary, easily leads a man to do some little more, which, in the aggregate, shall furnish abundance and content. And there is nothing more simple and natural than this progression. Upon this principle it is, that a labouring man is no poorer for a wife and children, if the price of his labour is adequate to their sustenance; and many of them

them have the wit to find this out. It is a common obfervation at Manchefter, that the manufacturers are never diftreffed, but when the provifions are at a low price.

It is a melancholy circumftance, that the hufbandman who is employed in the product of the firft great article of national fupport, fhould not receive that proportionable increafe of wages to which he is juftly entitled, and which has been received by every other kind of labouring man for fome time; the policy of bringing bread into the hands of all artificers at the eafieft rate, allows of no remiffion of the hardfhips of the hufbandry labourer, which in this country begin to refemble thofe of the Helotes amongft the Spartans of old; fequeftered and fcattered over the whole furface of the kingdom, without the benefit of that light which is communicated by affociation, their fufferings are unheeded, for their employers are in general of the moft obdurate of heart; in thofe of a more enlightened underftanding, there is not that readinefs to affift a man with a large family, from the parifh ftock, which humanity and found policy prefcribe, to prevent his becoming a parifh charge in the common mode; but indeed

deed it ought not to depend on caprice, the calls for seamen, soldiers, and labourers, are so urgent that it ought to be the favorite max- of the government to encourage marriages amongst the lower orders, by granting an allowance for every child, above the number which the father is not able to support, and to be continued, till the child was of age to earn as much as the annual allowance; some encouragement they should have, lest like the labouring husbandmen of a neighbouring kingdom, they should resolve not to marry; they find it necessary in France to encrease population by giving portions with young women in marriage, for the existence of the nation is connected with it.

To the many causes which have tended to increase the amount of the poor-rates, no person has been just enough to mention the low wages of the husbandman, though it is easily seen, that a man with three children can but scarcely supply them with bread only from his labour; but what is his situation if he is thrown out of employment for three or four weeks, how is he to recover that loss? to return from this digression;

The selfish influence so apt to predominate
in

in the nature of man, is no where so powerfully excited, as amongst a commercial people, who are generally so blinded by it, as scarcely ever to see their true interest; how many in this country are alarmed on hearing that another nation is getting forward in some particular manufactory, and wish that the whole world should depend on us for every thing they wanted, without reflecting that if there were no industry in other nations, there could be no demand for our goods, for they would not have the means of paying for them;* upon this sordid principle it is, that with all our riches, we deny ourselves the full enjoyment of the best French wines, to drench a dull sophisticated mess from Portugal ‡: if the French were encouraged to go more into vine-planting, we should have another market for our corn; in this the advantage would be on our side.

* It may be supposed that many have rejoiced at the situation of French affairs, without knowing that a civil war carried on for a few years, to the barbarous extent of which we have had some shocking instances, would bring many evils on this country; such a wheel as France taken out of the commercial engine for a short time, might derange the whole machinery, beyond our powers and art to adjust.

‡ Mr. Hume's Essays.

We shall now take a view of some of the most notorious evils, which the great influx of riches has had upon the morals and manners of the people of this country; it will require no depth of reflection, or keen observation, for the marks are visible in almost every class; it is indeed a natural consequence, attested by many examples in history, that every nation enriched by an over extensive Commerce, has in the possession of its riches, lost its vigour and virtue, and sunk into ruin and slavery.

The insatiable thirst of riches is almost universal amongst us, to be rich is to be every thing; the instances that might be found of parents clearing their houses of their whole progeny to ship them for India, are numerous; unhappy parents! to have so entirely extinguished in their bosoms all moral and physical sensibility, as to banish their offspring from their sight for ever! for the few who return from climates so little congenial with northern constitutions, make the expectations of meeting again, almost hopeless. We should be glad to awaken some to reflection, whom the frequency of the measure, amongst others, might lull into a forgetful-
ness

nefs of the fhame, which fhould attend fuch a deviation from Nature's dictates, as the fending young gentlewomen from their native refidence; it is againft every fenfe of female decorum, that they fhould be doomed to encounter the dangers of the feas, and the difafters of foreign climates; it would be a cruel injuftice to caft the leaft reflection on thofe amiable young perfons, who are without blame in confenting to become the victims to the unbounded avarice of their infatuated and unfeeling parents.

The extravagance in drefs among the lower orders of both fexes, the depredations on the coin of every fpecies, the increafe of fuicides, thefts, robberies, cheatings of all kinds, and murders, are fome of the confequences of a great increafe of riches. Many circumftances have co-operated to relax the morals of the people, which a watchful government might have prevented, but we are conftrained to infift, that in fome cafes the people are abandoned to the fulleft temptation by the deliberate determination of the legiflature: a reformation of manners would reduce the revenue, and who is fo blind as not to fee, that if the malt-tax, and taxes on spirits are to furnish as much as they now do, that a certain portion of hemp will necessarily be employed?

The debasement of the coin is a heavy tax, the quantity of light gold is prodigious, since the last coinage; those who are fifty years of age only, may remember when there was no light gold, there's a morsel for reflection! now there is no silver or copper that is unadulterated, and we may soon be forced to follow the Chinese mode; in China they have no coin, every payment there is made in bullion, decided by the scales and weights; it is hoped for the honour of the nation, that we may do our business without such a stigma which would be nothing short of a proclamation to the whole world, that we are a nation of scoundrels.

Montesquieu has delivered it as a maxim, that, "Commercial states may get to a pitch of mediocrity and continue there for a long time, because the advances being gradual, are unnoticed; but when once their grandeur is become so clear, that there is no avoiding to see its effects, every nation will strive to deprive it of advantages they conceive to have been taken of them by surprize." Is it a question

queſtion that there is a country at this time the envy of all the nations in Europe, and the example to ſpur them on to an imitation of that, which may give them a portion of its ſpoils, and tumble it down.

An exceſs of trade can never be permanent, the competition of other nations will make it ſtagnate, and the great miſchief that would befall that ſtate, when its trade was again reduced to mediocrity, would ariſe from the manners of its people ; it would then be ſeen that the true opulence of a country is in its manners, and not in its riches.

When the flux of riches into Rome began to ebb, it was obſerved by Salluſt, " That it is difficult to be a good citizen with riches above a private ſtation; but with deſires and regrets for what has been enjoyed, and is loſt, a man is ready for all manner of wickedneſs : thoſe among the Roman people who had no patrimony, could not bear to ſee it in others."

To bring a people back to good habits which they have once deſerted, is the moſt difficult taſk of Legiſlature ; we can eaſily find an inſtance that it requires a cruel in‑

difference only, to fuffer a people to grow vicious, and to be ready to punifh them. *Facilis defcenfus averni ; fed revocare gradum!*

If a nation has more of its people unhappy, even during its full poffeffion of riches from an abundant Commerce, than were in its ftate of mediocrity,* we muft confefs that in all the purfuits of weak-fighted mortals, there is none more vain and illufory than unbounded trade. But the ftone is now rolling down the hill with fuch accumulated force and velocity, that no human means can ftop it.

In the precarious ftate of this country, from its enormous debt, many events may be forefeen that would put it in a deplorable fituation, in one particular, beyond what any other nation has fuffered. One thing is in our favour, as Commerce introduced riches, the good fenfe of the country has, by a peculiar felicity, been heightened and diffufed beyond what any other ever experienced; in this we build our hopes, that when the aggregate ingenuity of the people, fhall be the moft powerfully exerted, it may be equal to the overcoming every calamity.

* We have no doubt but that Mr. Pitt has ten applications to one, that Sir Robert Walpole, had fifty years ago.

ESSAY VIII.

Of POLITICS AND POLITICIANS.

————*Nec jura fidemque,*
Respectumque Deum nunquam speraveris aulæ.
LUCAN.

Virtue or Truth at Court let none expect,
Where plighted faith and oaths, they all neglect.

THE science of Politics, so far as it relates to the public institutions and government of any particular state is easily obtained, and the result of its maxims is to be found in the past and present time, subject however, as every thing sublunary is, to mutability; it must necessarily also be different in every state from the nature of the laws, religion and customs; but in all its great objects, whether it be commerce, or alliances for a mutual defence with other countries, there can be nothing

thing for a long time equivocal, nothing which is not feen, felt and underftood by all parties concerned; and whether it be to make an equal partition of advantages or difadvantages from intervening accidents, if there be a difpofition to do juftice, there will be no occafion given for plots or counterplots.

The famous treaty fo foon compleated between England and Holland, by Sir William Temple and De Witt, furnifhes us with an example of what may be done where fincerity is the bafis; as fome fplendid meetings of ambaffadors and plenipotentiaries may do of the contrary, where many months have been fpent in fettling their precedence, and fuch like impertinences, while all parties were waiting to feize fome advantages in violation of the preliminaries, from the fuccefs of an army in the field, or fleet at fea; in thefe cafes, ambition, the private intereft of the prince, or generally fomething remote from the welfare of the country, whofe minifter plays this game, is found to guide the operation.

If we take a view of our political conduct fince the revolution, we fhall be able at the fame time to fathom the wifdom of the French, who like ourfelves are overwhelmed with

debts

debts unneceffarily contracted; the common obfervation that the French rank above us in political knowledge and in negotiation, is ridiculous; the difference is in the national manners more than in wifdom; they fquander great fums of money through affectation, and will fometimes rifk truth and good fenfe, for the appearence only of accquiring advantages by addrefs; what could fineffe atchieve againft a man like Cromwell, who faw his intereft and was fteady to his purpofe? Richlieu whofe food was cabal, and intrigue, was forced to yield to a well fupported bluntnefs. Suppofe that when the general terms for a peace are fettled, a political dabbler will reckon it clever to chicane for fome alteration in his favour, if he finds out that the other party will fubmit to a trifling impofition rather than retard the grand object; the advantage which feems to be gained by fuch conduct, is fure to be overpaid in fome fubfequent bufinefs; but the man who is greedy of being thought a politician, thinks nothing of a future reftitution.

The French, from the nature of their government, are more employed in court cabals than fuits the difpofition of our countrymen, and

and are trained to a management of themselves, neceffary perhaps in a country where every man is in the habit of foliciting protection from fomebody above him; court maxims have there a more univerfal influence than with us, which is one reafon why every Frenchman affumes the character, and believes himfelf a politician: the little intrigues employed to obtain the fmiles of a prince, however they may fometimes lead to a decifion of importance, deferves not the name of Politics, but of cunning; it may be allowed that the practice at home prepares a man for the like cabals in a foreign court, where the fame kind of manners prevail; and thus far the Frenchman has a fuperiority over an Englifhman, but this can do but little in a treaty of ferious concern.

A Frenchman may be faid to labour in his vocation while he is intermedling and endeavouring to conduct affairs, in which he naturally has no concern. In Monfieur Savary's Account of Egypt one may fee this principle averred, and alfo that it is foftered by the minifter at home on all occafions, even to a great expence. With what fervour the French in America leagued themfelves with

with the Indian tribes, marrying and settling themselves with animals who could barely be allowed to make a part of the human kind! this was however a gratification to a Frenchman, because he believed it Politic, and himself a Politician.

Of our national politics it may be asserted, that it is impossible to show in what manner the welfare of this country has been seriously concerned in any of the great wars in which it has taken a part, since the revolution, if we except that of 1755, on account of the incroachments by the French on our American territories; which in the end was managed with the same dereliction of the interests of the people, with all the former wars, and the same prostitution of good sense; the opposite conduct of the same man, when in and and out of power, displayed the limits of patriotism so eminently, that a proper return for public confidence, is scarcely ever to be again expected; indeed the principles of our constitution are now so generally overlooked, that we do not exact it from the minister, that he shall be the friend of the people, and he has at length attained his just and emphatical title, of being the "King's minister."

In king William's reign it was complained of in parliament as a grievance, that by the innovation of a junto, called a cabinet council, the privy council, a conſtitutional inſtitution was joſtled out of its province; but how in our days if the cabinet council is aſſembled only like the former parliaments in France, to regiſter the kings edicts? it has been frequently announced in the public papers, that in ſome late political buſtles, that all diſpatches were firſt carried to the king, and not as formerly was the rule, to the ſecretary of ſtate's office; we do not know that this new practice which in a manner annihilates the ſecretary of ſtate's office, is founded in the nature of our conſtitution, even in the opinion of an honeſt tory, but we know that it is very cónſiſtent in ſuch governments as Pruſſia.

From the beginning of this century to the preſent time, it has been the conſtant practice, under one or other futile pretence, to gratify the reigning prince with the diſpoſal of the blood and treaſure of the nation, to poize the jarring intereſts of German princes, or countervail French intrigues; to overlook our inſular ſituation, and to perſuade the people that their ſafety was concerned in what
might

might befal Bavaria or Auftria; at one time this fyftem has been fweetened to their palates, by the profpect of an increafe of Commerce; and at another, working upon the generous fpirit of the nation to take a part, vifibly againft its interefts and judgment.

It may be thought ftrange, that the Politics of a government, fo univerfally efteemed to have its foundation in the fecurity and welfare of the people, fhould never have extended its wifdom to the granting a few hundred thoufand pounds, for the fettling fome induftrious poor families on the wafte lands, for the increafe of population and agriculture; whilft fo many millions have been raifed, in which neither the minifter or the people had any expectation of the national interefts being concerned in the application of the money. If we compare the profits of our commerce, great as they are, with the amount of the annual intereft of fuch part of the national debt as has been incurred by wars and other means, under pretence of its encouragement, it would feem that we are a nation of merchants whofe pride it is to trade without profit; we allow that many families have been enriched, but how does this counterpoize

terpoize the evil of the national debt, which affects the economical management of every houshold in the kingdom. As we have no longer the means of displaying such quixotism as formerly, it might be expected that our politics should assume an appearance more cautious and intelligible.

The business of a nation is guided by the prevalence of whim or wisdom, as it may happen, just like the concerns in private life, of lesser moment. In society, the best defiance to censure, is to be able to say that we do but as others do, and it is to be presumed, that the grand councils of this nation have been often stimulated to pursue measures, foreign to the political interests of the kingdom, because the French had set the example: if Monsieur Dupleix had not shown us the way to sovereignty in India, it is probable that the native modesty of the merchants of Leadenhall-Street, might have prevented them from presuming to dispose of crowns and empires, and that they might have been content in their station of traders; there is no doubt but our adoption of this further plan, will be manifested by the same effects, which measures so unjust and unwise have always produced;

duced; we have already many evils to encounter on that account, and it would be no difficult tafk to demonftrate, that empire in India never was, nor ever can be, beneficial to any nation in Europe; for a late inftance we could name the Portuguefe; we could name another country whofe trading interefts are finking every year, from the expences of fuch diftant poffeffions, and which no human wifdom can prevent.

If we had left the French to their political interference with the eaftern potentates, and directed our national exertions to the fecurity of our commerce only, we fhould have been in a better fituation, as far as relates to the happinefs and welfare of the nation; with the profits of half a million a year only, gained by commerce, the nation would have been more enriched, than from the importation of millions by other means; therefore the fooner we are driven to the fea fide, into our warehoufes, the better: we are not however ignorant of the little refpect that will be paid to fuch reafoning.

The underftanding of the nation has been infulted with hearing India called the chief fupport of this country, at the fame time that

that the people were taxed to raife a buttrefs for this column of fecurity,—the minifter felt its fupporting influence.

In the profecution of ftudies belonging to a good education, young men eafily conceive high notions concerning men in exalted ftations, and of the irkfome and laborious avocations of a minifter of ftate, whofe head they believe to be always teeming with fome wife project for the good of the ftate; the fon of count Oxenfteirn, who by his father had been appointed to a place of great truft and profit, expreffed his earneft defire to decline the acceptance of it, on the fcore of his incapacity, "Oh my fon, faid the count, you little know with how fmall a portion of underftanding, the world is governed," and in all countries it is a kind of maxim, that a man is proper for any employment he can procure; we cannot omit a ftory told by the earl of Stair, who had been embaffador in France, that when at Paris, being in great favour with the duke of Orleans who was regent, he was one morning admitted into his bedchamber; the duke was in bed with his miftrefs, and his favourite L'Abbe du Bois was prefent; the duke faid to him, laughing

very

very heartily, "we are on ſtate buſineſs, my lord, and I have admitted you, that you might ſee how the affairs of a large empire may be tranſacted."

If the knowledge of the Political intereſts of nations, and the government of them, are in all places at variance, we muſt conclude that the ſcience of Politics alone, does not make a Politician, we ſhall endeavour therefore to ſhow what does: The hiſtories of thoſe who have been diſtinguiſhed as the greateſt Politicians in Europe, degrade human nature to a degree that is difguſtful; they appear to have been men, hardened by the commiſſion of the blackeſt crimes, ſo as to be familiar with perfidy, aſſaſſination, poiſon, perverſion of the laws, and every vice that belongs to the character of the moſt deteſtable villains; but as our manners are leſs ferocious than formerly, if we ſhould, in the language of chemiſtry, decompoſe a Politician of the preſent day, we ſhould diſcover ſuch qualities as theſe, in the component parts, " with a mind embarraſſed and a clouded viſage, he is ſupple and inſinuating, always diſſimulating; having two or three countenances at command, never thinking that he ſays, or ſaying
what

what he thinks; unjuſt, without pity, and at all times ready to ſacrifice any portion of the human race, to whatever may be neceſſary to his political career;"

We know they're ſo in France, in Spain, and Rome, God knows if we have better folks at home.

A Politician would feel himſelf degraded if we ſhould attribute to him ſuch vulgar principles as honour and probity; he will allow, that they are neceſſary on certain occaſions, but that civil and political morals are different things, that in the wide range of political wiſdom, morality muſt give way; preſerving however the appearance of it, if it may be, which he thinks preferable to the thing itſelf, as it ſhows his powers of deception, which he conſiders as his moſt flattering point of view. It may not be wholly extravagant to make an obſervation here, that a court, which naturally ought to be the ſanctuary of virtue and truth, ſhould be the ſoil where the arts of deception flouriſh moſt, and are brought to the higheſt perfection.

In the common acceptation, to be a man of low cunning is to be of a debaſed character, but to be called of conſummate policy, is to rank above human nature; and yet it would be difficult to point out the difference, but in the found.

The pretended knowledge of the world in the political hemifphere, confifts in this fhort comprehenfive maxim, " That all men are rafcals." Minifters of ftate, who are engaged in the moft fecret concerns, and the moft interefting to the parties who tranfact the bufinefs, may often meet with fome who work with the fame tools as themfelves; in thefe trials of fkill, they learn to harden their hearts, and acquire an indifference to every thing that does not contribute to their ambition and intereft.

We do not prefume to recommend any thing to thofe who manage the bufinefs of a nation, but to their admirers, who publifh the golden rule we have mentioned, we think it may not be amifs for them to examine their own principles of action; if the refult of fuch inquiry be a purity of mind, they will entertain fo much refpect for others, as to believe there are many of that defcription; for a man to perfuade himfelf that he alone is juft, is more than any felf-conceit can warrant; on the other hand, if he finds the maxim

L admiffible

admissible, he should be cautious of the promulgation, because the assertion, however it is meant to imply a recondite and refined observation, is known by the wise to be taken up at random, and to be a very loose definition of human moral conduct.

It is amusing to observe the affectation of those who are of the lower departments in the *Corps diplomatique*, or other ministerial bustle; they look at a man as if they were possessing themselves of his most concealed thoughts, covering their countenances with reserve, and their speech with hesitation. If these diminutives were to appear with a frank and cheerful behaviour, they would dwindle into mere ordinary men. This, perhaps, may be admitted as a standard for the measuring every man's political stature, in such situations, " That in proportion to his want of good sense, and power, he puts on the appearance of cunning, or stateliness;" perhaps no man was ever seen to return from a Political employment abroad, with the same plainness of manners he sat out with.

ESSAY

ESSAY IX.

Of RELIGION.

Sponte sua sibi quisque valere, et vivere doctus.
                                                        JUVENAL.

Whate'er is best, each for himself may know,
And all be right, though different roads they go.

THERE is nothing more absurd and illiberal, than the unkind conclusions that some men presume to draw against those who may chance to differ from them in religious concerns; from which every man should reasonably be exempt: it was otherwise with the ancients, the nature of whose religion was of another cast from ours. In those times, enthusiasm was a vapour so cold in its operations, that it was necessary to affift it with copious draughts of wine, and objects of gaiety.

Within the laft eighteen hundred years, to enumerate the evils which have been brought into the world on the fcore of religion, is fcarcely poffible; there is no excefs of cruelty or folly that could debafe our nature, that has not been practifed, and there never can be any thing happen in the world, to fhow the turpitude of mankind fo completely, as when under the influence of religious fury.

Tantum relligio poterit fuadere malorum.*
Luc.

The millions that are now exifting in Europe, equal not the number of thofe who have been deftroyed, by all the methods made ufe of, under pretence of filling the duties of a Religion, faid to be conferred through the mercies of a juft and benevolent deity, to be the happinefs and confolation of mankind through this life. The Chriftian Religion, had never more the appearance of a prefent from heaven than now, that it has put off fo many abfurdities that were of human inftitution.

* Religion only could produce fuch ills.

The pope, who was formerly the chief engineer, is now become an old goffip that the generofity of an enlightened age permits to enjoy a princely revenue, impofed by the arts of his predeceffors on the ignorance of the times; he remains now rather an incitement to moderation in religious matters, the force of his anathemas is gone, and his bleffings are received as reciprocal civilities.

There yet however remains enough of the leaven of religious difcord in all the countries of Chriftendom, to be the reproach of a philofophical age; we have more generally acquired the means of following our religious duties, without infulting others of a contrary perfuafion, than moft other countries.

It may be received as a maxim, that every man who boaftingly fets himfelf above others in a religious conduct, is a fool, or knave, and this conclufion is not ungenerous, for why fhould any man endeavour to impofe that upon me, which may be only pretence, and of which I am incompetent to judge? the rule of faith of one man, can never reafonably be the concern of another; whether his actions be generous and equitable, is of confequence to fociety, but on fubjects purely of reflection,

reflection, as how a perfon fhall endeavour to make himfelf an object of divine favour, who fhall prefume to decide for him?

If a mode of affembling and addreffing the the deity, is fixed upon by the wifdom of the legiflation, for the guidance of thofe who may be fuppofed to want direction, it is the duty of every one to fubmit to it, as far as his confcience will allow him; but if another way of thinking, or even the vanity of diffenting, fhould incline fome to adopt another method, it fhould be done modeftly, without arrogating to themfelves more wifdom or piety.

The vulgar and ignorant who are unacquainted with inquiry and profound fcience, have commonly a contempt for philofophy; they have a fcepticifm arifing from their ignorance, which makes them reject every principle that is fubmitted to reafon, and they rivet themfelves the fafter, in proportion to the abfurdity of what they adopt, by which they fave themfelves trouble, and are convinced as far as they wifh to be; "they know not that faith is a fpecies of reafon, and that Religion is a branch of philofophy, the truth of which is eftablifhed by a train of arguments,

and

and its principles difcovered in the fame progreffive manner, as thofe of Politics, or Phyfics."*

Thofe are ufually the moft prefumptuous, who have reflected the leaft concerning the nature of their religion; content with thinking that above comprehenfion which requires reflection, they make it up by a vigour of belief, agreeably to their notions of belief.

They who enter into ftudy and inquiry, find nothing too difficult as a fubject of difcuffion, though abfolute conviction fhould be denied; they know the narrow limits of the mind of man, they fee its infufficiency to decide on things that are the objects of the fenfes, and the fubjects of daily practice, as well as in fuch more remote from experience: the cohefion and compofition of the parts of ftones and marbles, the growth of plants, and the whole proceedings of nature, are inexplicable; but that fhould not deter us from an exertion of our capability to be acquainted with every thing within the fcope of our comprehenfion.

There are many things in the myftical

* Locke.

part of Religion, which are not alike eafy to be inveftigated by all underftandings, however ardent the defire may be to coincide with whatever is offered as matter of conformity in faith; but it would be unjuft in the higheft degree to fay, that he who takes pains to find the truth, he that endeavours to make the object of his adoration the moft confiftent with his reafoning faculties, is blameable, and that the indifferent lazy believer, ought to be efteemed the more religious. One fees a light in the road, at a diftance, in the night, and thinks it to be within fome houfe; another lefs fatisfied, rides that way to afcertain the fact, and upon a clofe infpection, finds it to be a vapour of that kind, called *Ignis fatuus*, or Will-o'-the wifp, ought he to be reprobated for that?

Every perfon holds all religious opinions in fome fort of contempt, fave thofe he has adopted; it may happen that one in the purfuit of a Religion fuited to his mode of faith, may differ from all, and every fect on the furface of the earth; fome may reckon him very faftidious, but the truth is, that he is only at variance with one Religion more than his neighbour; and this is no great matter on a

fubject

subject of such a nature, that it is rarely seen that any two persons can make themselves understood by each other, in the definition and exposition of their ideas concerning some subjects of belief; for which reason, no person of good sense and decorous behaviour, whether layman or divine, ever examines another on such topics; a man can no more believe some things, of which he may desire to be persuaded, than he can lift a weight disproportioned, to his bodily strength. There are many who have something about them they think a Religion, which came upon them they know not how: In such a vacancy of mind, a system may no doubt be planted and cherished for its novelty.

It has happened more than once, that only one man in the world was right on a particular subject, as in the case of him who first promulgated his opinion of the earth's motion: in Religion we have seen many things discussed, concerning which, we are positive no man can be right; which is indeed of no great consequence, if the opinion, however distant from the commonly received sense of the thing, is not backed with violence, or framed to hurt the peace of mind of others.

What signifies it which way a man thinks on subjects incomprehensible? or, who can know more of a man's thoughts than he discloses, or even the sincerity of that?

One says, he takes the Religion as instituted by government, for the rule of faith and happiness of the people; another says, this was put together in times less enlightened than ours, and that he may justly reject such things as are repugnant to his understanding; he perceives some things which, to his mind, agree neither with the sense, nor letter of the original; some things foisted in by different councils, to answer political purposes, at those periods for which they were calculated.

A right reverend and learned prelate has said more in defence of revealed Religion in a few words, than is to be met with in some cart loads of folios*. " He who finds his endeavours to comprehend the works of creation, checked at every turn; who understands that every the minutest part of this little earth, which is itself nothing as it were, when compared with the infinity of the divine

* Dr. Watson's Chemical Essays, Vol. 1. Pa. 89.

works, is to him one great miracle, will not be over zealous in affirming, that God cannot interfere by his providence, in the management of what he hath made, or that he has interfered in this or that particular way. In the confcious abafement of his own intellect, which philofophy will have taught him, he will be cured of all attachment to fyftem, whether it be a fyftem of bigotry or infidelity : he will not be fond of anathematizing every one who cannot think with him in religious matters ; nor on the other hand, will he contend that a revelation from God muft be an impoffibility, from any abftract notions he may have framed of the nature and works of the fupreme Being."

So long as Religion fhall be fubmitted to the infpection of reafon, its fituation will be fluctuating, and if the interference of reafon is excluded, it may become ridiculous: when the Chriftian Religion was moft flourifhing, fuperftition was employed to take every advantage of the credulity and ignorance of mankind; if it has fince affumed another face there is nothing to be wondered at, it is in the progreffive order of things. The Religion of the Roman people, from the time of
Tullius

Tullius Hoſtilius, to that of Julius Ceſar and Cicero, went through a great change from the improvement of the human underſtanding: it may be ſaid that the Religion of ancient Rome, was of human contrivance, Be it ſo.

Let any one examine the writers of queen Elizabeth's reign, and from their authority, let him analize the manners of the nobility and gentry of that era, and it will be found, that in reſpect of all thoſe qualifications which are the ornaments of our nature, that the middle order of people at this time, are more humanized, and poſſeſs a greater variety of knowledge: the ſame improvement is to be traced in all the arts and ſciences, which having been brought under ſtronger powers of reflection, reaſoning and experience, muſt neceſſarily produce a great variety of more refined opinions.

To ſome it may ſeem that we argue againſt all Religion, when we ſay that every one muſt judge for himſelf; nothing as been ſaid againſt the Religion of this country as it now goes, and woe betide thoſe who would diſturb it; however ſome may think, there is no piety where there is no diſcord; for the other part, if it has not been ſhown that every perſon

son in the habits of reflection, muſt determine for himſelf, and abide by his own peculiar mode of thinking, there has been a great loſs of argument, ſuch as it is.

But where is the difficulty in ſuppoſing a nation to be without any particular mode of worſhip, and that the laws and power of the magiſtrate, ſhall keep good order in the ſtate, without any Myſteries of Religion? if we are not miſinformed, the great empire of China, anſwers ſuch deſcription exactly; many are there found who to ſhow their ingenuity, we may ſuppoſe, make an open profeſſion of atheiſm, ſome follow Confucius, ſome the Religion of the grand Lama; but as deep reaſoning is not the produce of any ſoil or climate, we may conclude, that the greater part live in a total indifference on the ſubject of Religion: we believe that in Holland, however famous for toleration, that the preachers of the Religion of the ſtates, are under the ſubordination of the magiſtrate, and are very ſedulouſly watched, as to the ſubjects of their diſcourſes.

They who contend that the people of this country have relaxed in their morals of late years, are wide of the mark in ſuppoſing it

to

to be the effect of infidelity; the cause is to be found in a variety of circumstances that must ever accompany a great influx of riches into a country; infidelity is only a component part of the extraneous mass of corruption, that it drags along with it; we speak of that vulgar species of infidelity which is adopted to countenance vice; but as even that must be built on some argument and reflection, it can never be widely diffused amongst the lower order of people, who are vicious from habit, ignorance, and the want of care in the magistrate.

An elegant writer of late times, has prescribed a certain period for the existence of the Christian Religion, as the principal system of worship in Europe; but as no objection can be brought against its moral part, it is likely to be very slow in its decline: if the arts and sciences should sink into oblivion, and chaos come again, it may then have to encounter a new system of mythology, and whether in such a conflict it shall rise superior, no one can pretend to guess.

It appeared to the warm imagination of Rousseau, that the Tartars will infallibly conquer Europe at some distant period; and if

he

he had continued his prophecy, he might have said that the Chriſtian Religion, would then give way to that of the grand Lama.

ESSAY

ESSAY X.

Of POLITENESS.

Non aliter manifesta putans abscondere mentis,
Quam gaudiis.
                              LUCAN.

Lest the rude passions should the truth reveal,
He learns with smiles, his anguish to conceal.

POLITENESS is the assimulation of our behaviour to the practice of all those qualities that form the most refined pleasures of social intercourse, the appearance of universal benevolence, generosity, modesty, and of making our own happiness spring from the accomodation of others.

French Politeness, so called, consists in an active distribution of civility to every one in company,

company, though not quite impartially proportioned; in this country it feems rather confined to a quiet unaffuming conduct, that is intended to give no offence ; the manners of the two nations make the difference, and is the reafon they are each undervalued by the other. The difficult and fublime part of Politenefs, is, to behave fo, that we fhall make others fatisfied with us, and with themfelves.

The activity of the French gentleman in the practice of his complaifance, in which he is not fo rude as to neglect himfelf, requires more art than an Englifhman can perfuade himfelf to ufe ; but that which appears in this cafe as a bufinefs, is meerly the effect of early habit : a polite education in France is fo uniform in its effects, that it refembles a public inftitution, every man is an epitome of the nation; boys were a few years fince dreffed in full-trimmed cloaths, fwords and bags, at fix years of age, and began that cajolery with the ladies, which was to be the pride of their lives.

It is not thirty years fince every gentleman made Paris his conftant refidence, and was full dreffed his whole lifetime; a little since that time, an essay was made of walking the streets in the morning in a frock and boots, *a l'Angloise*; and however trifling such a beginning may appear, it has probably been the first step to that wonderful change in the national manners; the morning emancipation from the chariot, was like the letting a bird out of its cage, his walks brought him accquainted with many things that would have been hidden from him during life; it increased his ideas by the introduction of a more familiar intercourse with mankind in general, than formal societies admit of; and being one half of the day disincumbered of forms and senseless ceremonies, he might be imperceptibly led to entertain notions of general freedom; for at that time the French gentry lived in their particular coteries, or societies, strangers to that extended communication of ideas in use here. To return from this digression.

The Spaniards, who are remarked for entertaining high respect for honorable and fair dealing, admit, however, some grimace in their civilities; it is reckoned polite to make an offer of a horse, or any thing that may excite some compliment from a person in company; but the acceptance of it, would in their

their opinions, betray such a total want of good breeding, as to excuse the taking no further notice of the offer.

Lord Chesterfield used to say, that if the good people in courts were not to smile upon each other, they must stab; this may be true, but it is a curious account of the peace and harmony that reign in the minds of those, whose fortunes and elevated stations enable them to attain all the happiness that our nature is capable of enjoying.

In towns, the inhabitants practice more outward civility than villages; and in the capital, they learn by an interchange of ingenuity, to envelope their minds with so many coverings, that what they say or do, may be no true criterion of their minds and inclinations.

Where the interference and jar of interests, however trifling, are constant, it is difficult to find three persons in such situation, agreeing for a month together, unless there may chance to be one amongst them, endowed with a more than common share of good sense, or kindness of disposition: so in private families, and the larger community of village society, where each is conftantly under the eye of the other, there is no fcope for diffimulation; and therefore a long continued harmony is not frequent: it is found neceffary in the great intercourfe of mankind, to affume thofe virtues which they have not, and where they only touch and go, there feems to be no delufion.

It is poffible to live in the practice of all the amiable and focial virtues, which we call Politenefs, and at the fame time to make ufe of the pureft fincerity in all our dealings. A good underftanding, generofity of temper, and a philofophical difpofition, muft unite, to form this character; which is fo beneficial to fociety, that it challenges a higher title, than that of being meerly polite.

ESSAY

ESSAY XI.

L'ENNUI.

> ———————*Quòd petis hic est :*
> ———*Animus si non te deficit æquus.*
> Hor.

Whate'er you seek, you every where may find,
If sweet content is pilot to the mind.

ENNUI is a French word almost naturalized amongst us, to express which, we have no word in our language exactly synonymous. In the French language Ennui signifies languor, lassitude, fatigue of the mind caused by something displeasing in it self, or by its continuance, or by the disposition one may be in ; it signifies also chagrin, care and regret, the Ennuis of old age; but it is in the first sense it is generally used

used amongst us, and for which, when we substitute low spirited or splenetic, we use terms more than adequate to express our meaning; for these are sometimes serious constitutional defects, not easily put off; whereas the other requires the absence only, perhaps of a particular person, or thing, or some matter equally trifling.

Ennui is a disease to those who indulge themselves in fastidiousness upon every occasion to such a degree, that they are disgusted with every thing they see, and live in a constant fretting and uneasiness at things which are overlooked by a mind in harmony with itself; some are unhappy at the dishes on a table being placed contrary to their taste, at any defect in the dress or manners of those in company; when in town they sigh for the country, and when there, despise every object that presents itself.

This uncomfortable habit of mind is rather an object of ridicule than commiseration, for it grows out of an abundant possession of the means of contentment; those who have real cares have no room for the entertainment of such a guest; it is nursed only where the business of life is, what is termed pleasure,

pleasure, and amongst such, there are few men who have been deep enough in philosophical reflection, to find out, that to live in a round of uninterrupted delight, is not the lot of any one person in the world.

Those who are engaged in business know of no such refinements; they are pleased when not really troubled, are content because they think little about it, and find their happiness in the common cases and commodities of life; but as uneasiness and cares seem to be the inevitable destiny of all, we see that those whose situations are so fortunate as to exclude a large portion, are, as it were, forced to an exertion of their ingenuity, to supply as much uneasiness as shall put them upon par with others.

There is nothing more difficult of attainment than the knowledge of making the most of life; and yet it is never considered as a necessary instruction: every person is left to find it out as they can; the necessity of employing the mind is common to all, and it is well known, that if its pursuits are not directed to something proper, it becomes languid, or the slave of folly and vice.

ENNUI.

Si non paret, imperat. *

HOR.

How many young men have gone into the ruin and extravagancies of play, from a defire only of filling up their vacant time; for want of being accuftomed from an early period to amufe themfelves with mufic, drawing, aftronomy, botany, agriculture, or the ftudy of fome fcience; without any particular view to excellence, but meerly to avoid the *Tædium Vitæ*, by having fomething at hand that is agreeable to purfue.

The man who is plagued with poverty has a better time than he who has riches, without a proper fenfe of the enjoyment of them, or than him who has no refources in his mind, but is left to chance, to furnifh whatever may prefent itfelf for his amufement.

Ennui proceeds, very often, from the perfon's expectation of fomething pleafurable, which he proudly thinks fhould naturally attend his fortune and fituation in life, and meet him halfway; he rejects the fimplicity which rural fcenes afford, becaufe there is nothing new or entertaining; whereas to one

* An abject flave, or a fell tyrant reigns.

of an easy disposition of mind, every place affords something worthy of observation; the top of a barren mountain is an object of speculation, as to its form, composition, or the prospect from it of the adjacent country.

The education of women, where properly managed, is very advantageous to them; in respect of furnishing the means, to prevent Ennui, those little employments of various kinds, that awaken their ingenuity, are an inexhaustible fund of calm delight; by an habitual entertainment of their minds, they arrive at that harmony of temper and disposition, which sets them so indisputably above those who pretend to be their lords and masters.

To deliver up one's peace of mind to the little incidents of life, to the inadvertencies and petty offences, that grow out of fortuitous circumstances, is to forsake every pretension to wisdom, and to be again childish, after the season is gone by.

ESSAY XII.

Of BIOGRAPHY.

Omne animi vitium tanto conspectius in se
Crimen habet, quanto major qui peccat, habetur.
                              JUVENAL.

If the offender is, or wise, or great,
We set his follies at a higher rate.

EVERY person who has received the benefit of education, must consequently form opinions of the men and actions presented to his view in the course of his studies, and adopt partialities in favour of those whose characters are the subjects of his speculation and reflection, either as matter of admiration, or examples worthy of his imitation; in both cases he wishes to realize as far as he can, the facts recorded of them by searching for the best authenticated accounts, as on those he regulates the standard of their several merits.

Young men easily receive the first impressions with respect to the excellencies of a character; in a warriour they dwell with delight on the contemplation of his heroic courage and fortitude; and being unacquainted with envy and deceit in themselves or others, they never mistrust the most hyperbolical accounts, till at length, time and an acquaintance with the world shows them, that the difference between one man and another is not quite so disproportioned as they believed; and when they find that the great objects of their partiality had foibles, and some of them, vices too, and that all pretensions to greatness, may honestly be suspected to have some counterpoize of weakness, they acquire an addition of confidence to their own hopes of emulating such a character; and this reverse of the medal is as useful to the improvement of their talents, as the holding up the very extreme of excellence to their imitation.

To arrive at the eloquence of a Demosthenes, or a Cicero, or at the generalship of Cefar or Alexander, appears so unattainable to common capacities, that it even keeps down emulation; but when the student has observed that a man may excel in a particular art or science, but that no man is paramount in all things, he can allot to himself some place in society, of a subordinate degree to those sublime characters, which may be useful to his country, and sufficiently honorable to himself.

If it were possible to produce instances of great brilliancy of character without great inconsistencies of behaviour, it might be pardonable to reject the slight blemishes which make a part of a true description; but as we know it is impossible for men engaged in great affairs from their station in life, to be at all times so employed, we are naturally desirous of being acquainted with their disposition of mind, when free from restraint; the origin of this curiosity is, that we may measure ourselves with them, where we can; and here, again, the greatest character will afford this consolation, that it was not productive of more happiness to its possessor, than may be found in situations unconnected with every hope of rising into public notice.

They

They who think it a severity to scrutinize the actions of a man who died with the reputation of great abilities, are too fastidious: for if justice is done, in stating his merits which challenge our respect, there is little reason why his failings should be suppressed, particularly if they have been notorious; his foibles are as the shades of a picture, which without them would be but a sketch, or imperfect resemblance. We readily pardon whim, low spirits, or absence of mind, in great poets, mathematicians, or other learned or studious men, where an abstract way of thinking, together with their sedentary life are apt to derange the machine, and divert the mind from the little necessary offices so requisite to be attended to in society; but when we see great fortitude, clemency and generosity, exerted by the same man under the severest trials, we feel our nature humbled, and are vexed at the disappointment in finding him at another time, effeminate, cruel and sordid; but it is however the duty of the Biographer to record such inconsistencies: an erroneous estimation of human life, tends more to do mischief than good.

The writers of Dr. Johnson's life have undergone great obloquy, from those who are

very

very partial to his vaft endowments, but furely with unmerited rigour; the excefs of refpect in Mr. Bofwell was all but adoration, and certainly from the pureft motives; he he was content to exhibit himfelf as a mite, that he might fet off the gigantic appearance of his friend.

Mrs. Piozzi, with no lefs application of difcernment, and perhaps without the interference of malice, has ftrengthened the features of the picture by her manner of colouring, in laying on the fhades; but Dr. Johnfon's character is not hurt by either, nor are his great abilities difparaged beyond the common lot of men, exhibited in all points of view to the eyes of fevere criticifm; it was a faying of the great Conde, that no man was a hero, in the eyes of his valet de chambre.

*Nam nemo fine vitiis nafcitur ut æquum
Eft, cum fua compenfes vitiis bona.**

HOR.

Thofe who have feen Dr. Johnfon, as the writer of this has, in the full career of

* If in the beft fome faults are eafily found,
Let with due praife his virtues be renown'd.

happinefs,

happiness, which was in the conversation of
those who revered him, and to whom he was
ever ready to impart his knowledge with
the utmost complacency of humour, must
confess, that they never left his company
without improvement, admiration, and delight: those who knew him most intimately, had it both from observation and his own
confession, that his life was such a continual
torment from mental disease, that to get his
mind within his power, was the effort of the
most difficult of all struggles: against attacks
that nearly bereaved him of his senses, the
total deprivation of which, he often feared
would be his fate: but who is there among
the good and wise, that will think it any diminution of Dr. Johnson's fame, that he was
not always great; when he reflects on the vigour of that mind, which under such dread-
ful embarrassments, emitted those radiant
flashes, resembling the effulgence of lightning, whose splendour is the more dazzling,
when it bursts from the collision of the
blackest clouds. To his infirmity of mind,
the candid will impute the inefficacy of his fer-
vent piety, to yield him that consolation,
which a like practice ensures to others; and
pardon those peccadilloes, which like the

spots

spots in the sun, affect not the lustre of that luminary, and in no wise prevent the salutary operation of his other great qualities.

ESSAY

ESSAY XIII.

Of MARRIAGE AND GALLANTRY.

Nec Jovis illa meo thalamo præferret amori,
Nec me quæ caperet, non si Venus ipsa veniret,
Ulla erat, æquales urebant pectora flammæ.

OVID ME.

Had Jove made love his suit had been despis'd,
I my dear partner more than Venus priz'd;
The God of love had such kind flames bestow'd,
With equal ardour both our bosoms glow'd.

EPITHETS, in the extremes of good and bad, have been alike bestowed on the institution of Marriage; and as it is susceptible, of all the vast variety that the different dispositions can furnish, they may be severally applied, with some show of impartiality;

these

these however affect not the nature of the institution, which is so precious and necessary in every possible system of society, as to require no support from argument.

Marriage is in all respects equally commodious, from savage life, or the begining to adopt things convenient, by uniting the powers of intellect in a small number, to the higher attainments of civil life, which have sprung from a long exertion of wisdom in the many.

For as the well being of all societies is founded in the reciprocal advantages to all concerned, where can this bond of union begin so properly as between the sexes, formed by the great Author of our nature, to be alike attracting and attracted? and by what other means could the like advantages be so widely diffused, as by the operation of this compact, which in its fullest extent, might combine all the inhabitants of our globe in the same family?

It must however be allowed, that as matters are carried in refined society, marriage is a serious engagement, because every thing there is factitious; the difference of disposition

tion would do but little to disturb the quiet
of the parties concerned, where the neceffity of
mutual indulgence is fo apparent, if it were
not for the interference of extraneous things:
it is in fuch cities as London and Paris that
the inconveniences of Marriage, as they are
called, grow into a burden; but what elfe
is there of moral obligation, which is not
equally polluted by the influx of that predo-
minance of evil, which is fure to attend the
coalition of fuch large bodies of people? to
account for this, if we analize, as nearly as
we can, that heterogeneous animal, man, what a
mafs of contradiction do we find? and if
among the individuals we are forced to confefs, that generally fpeaking, a difpofition
to virtuous actions is not the moft prevalent,
what are we to expect from putting the con-
geries into fermentation? but how do friendfhips, juftice, humanity and every other efti-
mable quality, thrive amidft this jarring of
the elements?

Where Marriage is the effect of a mutual
inclination, where the eyes and heart have
been confulted, it is a law of nature which
nothing can abrogate, productive of a conftant

ftant fource of delights, unattainable by any other means.

It is an injuftice to charge the fair fex, whofe tafte is regulated by the men, with inconftancy in love, or thofe capricious changes of behaviour which make fuch irreparable breaches in domeftic happinefs; it is a rarity that the hufband does not lead the way, even where cuftom fanctifies the depravity of fuch conduct in both fexes: his education and former licentious courfes incline him to it.

The refpect for anceftry remaining in thofe countries, where fome feudal maxims exift, has a great influence in matrimonical connections; but is fo much extinguifhed here, that alliances by marriage which have the honour of family defcent only in view, are feldom preferred to riches; it may however be prefumed, that equality of rank and fortune, love out of the queftion, bids fairer to produce a more agreeable friendfhip, than an acceffion of riches, with an inferiority of birth and manners: to thofe who are indifferent to, and affect to defpife every thing in Marriage but riches, we fhall only fay that they have as much happinefs as they deferve.

Whenever

Whenever the despotism of fashion is allowed to prescribe that the pleasures of matrimony ought to be sacrificed to the pride of family and grandeur, there is a consistency in the attempt to degrade the worth of those qualities, which are so essential where love is the basis of the union; and even there the necessity intrudes itself, of establishing some mode of gratification, to counterbalance the loss of those comforts, abandoned by this perversion of nature's dictates: hence Gallantry, as it is termed in the language of politeness, or hypocrisy wrought into a system, to rob the most amiable part of God's work, of its greatest ornament, is accounted an elegant employment for a sensible man.

If in France the degeneracy of manners has at any time prevailed so far, as to make it a kind of reproach, according to the rules of politeness, for a husband to show a deference to his wife in public; and that on her part, the encouraging a more than common attention and regard from another man, shall have been admitted as becoming and proper, it is obvious that the substance is quitted for the shadow.

Our neighbours, the French, have for more than

than two centuries, been diftinguifhed for their fuperiority in the arts of gallantry; but if we beftow fome notice on their prefent manners, we fhall eafily difcern how little is to be gained by the dereliction of the pleafures, which belong to paying the tribute due to thofe amiable virtues in the fair fex, which is fo indefeafibly their right; and that where the greateft refinements of art have been employed to leffen their importance, it has always been found neceffary to fubftitute fomething in the behaviour of both fexes, which fhould reprefent them; for though it be a fafhion that every woman fhall wifh to be thought capable of infpiring a paffion in the breaft of fome other man than her hufband, yet the appearance of a chafte behaviour is not abandoned.

If, by the principles of French Gallantry, the women are allowed to have an univerfal power over tafte, in all its branches, and even in politics; if this afcendency extends even to the hufbands, it is not becaufe they are hufbands, but men: the authority allowed to the fex is clear of all tender fentiment and efteem; it obtains, becaufe it is an eftablifhed maxim that the quinteffence of politenefs is, to re-

refuse nothing to a woman; at the same time it is no less a part of the system, to despise them; and whosoever should divulge that he entertained an opinion more honorable to the sex, would be treated as a man who had no knowledge of them, but such as he had picked up in romances. As it was before observed that the men give the ton, or direct the taste of the fair sex, so it is seen in this case, that the women judge of themselves by the rules we have mentioned, thinking those who are inclined to esteem them, as unworthy of pleasing; from whence the man who is best received by them, *un homme de bonnes fortunes*, is always an impertinent coxcomb.

There is an unmanly frivolousness in this vice of Gallantry, which, it is to be hoped, will always prevent its being adopted to any great extent here; the support of the English free government, in which all the different ranks of gentry are so intimately concerned, keeps up provincial connections so far, as to make a constant residence in the metropolis, incompatible with such a system; for it is in the country that the higher orders lay the foundation of popular favour and distinction, by an observance of decorum in their behaviour;

viour; besides Gallantry is a farce which cannot be acted, but where it receives countenance from the authority of a powerful association, *defendit numerus.*

The attempts, from time to time, made here to introduce a refinement in Gallantry, show that we are not yet ripe to receive it; the characteristical mark of the nation, is to be in earnest in whatever engages the passions, and in Gallantry it is necessary to extinguish them.

Marriages, in England, are generally contracted with those views which are essentially necessary to produce happiness, and are as commonly successful as in any other country; nevertheless, without taking the pains to state the causes, we shall venture to assert, to the honour of our fair country-women, that good husbands, though no rarity, bear but a small proportion to the number of good wives.

M A X I M S.

There is nothing more difficult than to make a good choice of a husband, or wife.

If

If there is love, nature has made her choice; and without it, an union is generally attended with misfortunes and crimes.

There are so many conveniences neceſſary in Marriage, that it is folly to expect to find them all; it is proper however to secure the moſt important, thoſe which are natural; thoſe belonging to cuſtom, may moſtly be diſpenſed with by mutual agreement.

It is more conformable to reaſon that a man ſhould marry an inferior perſon, than a ſuperior; in the firſt caſe, he elevates his wife, in the other he degrades himſelf, without raiſing her: the ſociety of the family is regulated by the man who is the maſter of it; as his ſtate is, ſo will be the reſt.

It is in the order of nature that the wife obeys her huſband, therefore when he marries an inferior, the natural and civil orders are not violated, and all goes well; when he marries a ſuperior, he riſks his prerogatives, or is in danger of appearing ungrateful or contemptible.[*]

The

---

[*] When the Duke of Suffolk married Mary dowager Queen of France, the ſiſter of Henry the Eighth, on a Banner was wrote,

Cloth

The wife pretending to authority renders the master of the family the most ridiculous and miserable of Beings; like the favorites of the eastern despots, who are honoured and tormented by an alliance with the Sultan's family, he must creep into bed at the feet.

However difficult and delicate a man may be, it must be allowed that it is more becoming and pleasant to owe one's fortune to a wife, than a friend; in one case he is the protector, in the other the protected; but can a man have a better friend than his wife?

Figure in a woman is the first thing which strikes, it ought not to make the strongest impression, nor to be wholly overlooked.

It is hazardous to marry a great beauty, for though she may behave like an angel, she is always surrounded with enemies to herself, and her husband's peace; a few weeks reduces the value of her beauty in the eye of

> Cloth of Frize be not too bold,
> Tho' thou art match'd with Cloth of Gold.
> Cloth of Gold do not despise
> Tho' thou art match'd with Cloth of Frize.

The Gallantry of that age was unassuming.

her hufband, but the danger that may produce her unhappinefs remains.

Mediocrity in beauty, as in all other things, is to be preferred; an agreeable figure, infpiring good humour rather than love, is without prejudice to the hufband in every fenfe, and has advantages which turn to the common good: the graces do not wear out like beauty, but are inceffantly renewed; at the end of thirty years, fhe pleafes her hufband like the firft day.

There are only two claffes in both fexes, thofe who reflect, and thofe who do not; a man of either of thefe claffes, ought not to marry into the other: what a forrowful thing for a father of a family, who is of the thinking caft, to be married to a woman of an uncultivated mind, to whom he is unintelligible, conftrained to be fhut up within himfelf? how fhall a woman without reflection bring up her children? how teach them things of which fhe has no ideas? fhe has no means but careffes or threatnings, which will render them timid, or infolent: a fenfible man fhould therefore not marry a woman from a ftock, where good manners and good fenfe are not to be expected.

To continue lovers in Marriage, that is the art, to obtain this, there muft be but little conftraint, love and pleafure are free agents, and have wings; it is not poffeffion always which fatiates, it is fubjection: if you would be the lover of your wife, fhe muft be your miftrefs, and her own; the happy lover obtains all from refpect, nothing from duty, all the pleafure is derived from reciprocation.

The fociable relation of the fexes is wonderful; the wife learns of the hufband to fee what fhe ought to fee only, of the wife he learns to do what he ought; in the man are the principles, in the woman, the fpirit and the practical reafon, put them to their ufes: in the harmony, both are bettered, without knowing which has contributed moft; each is impelled by the other, and obeys, and both are mafters. In matters of council, the advice of a very fenfible woman is worth that of three very fenfible men: women have the art to fteer between the paffions, in a manner that men are ftrangers to; it is a peculiar prefent of nature.

A man can fcarcely love his children, who does not efteem his wife.

Thofe

Those who say that the sexes are equal, and their duties equal, know little of the matter; there are reciprocal duties, and duties peculiar to each sex, both of natural and civil institution.

Children are the grand cement of domestic content; thence arise fathers, mothers, brothers, sisters, these prevent the appearance of solitude, and the desire of going from home to be made gay and good humoured; this attraction at home, preserves a purity of manners, health and content.

ESSAY

ESSAY XIV.

Of TRUTH.

Æquum ac verum duxit, quod ipsi
Facere collibuisset.
Cic. in Sall.

Whate'er we like, or are inclin'd to do,
Is soon perceiv'd to be both right and true.

THE violation of Truth, open and avowedly, is so infamous that none will dare to profess the practice of it, as it disunites one man from another, and in the end would loosen the bands of society so as to destroy all intercourse; yet we adopt the various shapes, dresses, and accommodations of falsehood, under so many of its disguises, that we almost acknowledge that the shadow is equal to the substance.

The

The study of history is strenuously recommended to youth of all ranks of life above the mere vulgar, as a proper introduction to the inquiry concerning the nature of the human mind; as a mode to make them acquainted with facts, which sprung from causes that are likely again to have the same operations in the government to which they belong: but when a young person has carefully perused the histories of his own country, of other modern nations, and those of the ancients, if he is given to reflection, he may possibly be at a loss to guess, how the relations of so many murders, robberies, breaches of treaties, and other infractions of justice, and the praises bestowed on the successes attending them, can be usefully applied to a life of virtue and innocence.

If we admit the historical accounts, as containing the probability only of what might be transacted in like circumstances, it is, perhaps, of no great consequence, whether they are exactly true, or not; but it is safer to conclude, that nearly the whole is a tissue of errors, not absolutely contrived, to deceive indeed; but there is scarcely a fact, that is not in its nature simple, which is incontestably

contestably allowed to contain the whole that belongs to it. There are some lies, which, from prescription, acquire the force of Truth; Truths, which, by an exertion of ingenuity in after times, become falsehoods.

We could instance, in the history of England, some of the best authenticated facts, at one era, that in our days have been rendered problematical; nor are the histories of Greece and Rome secure from the introduction of novelties: those writers who lived so many ages nearer the eras in question, are treated as ignorant, or perverters of the truth; and indeed we must allow, that it is no more difficult to form probable conjectures concerning what might pass two thousand years ago, than of those things transacted only two hundred years since; and of such, history in general consists.

It is commonly asserted that the present time is not the hour to write the history of any transaction, in which a variety of persons and circumstances are involved; yet to a man of plain understanding, it would naturally appear, that of what he has seen, heard and read, concerning his own times, he may be as likely to understand as his great, great grandson;

fon; but it is urged that letters and papers, in private keeping, may hereafter bring things to light that are now myfterious. We have feen fuch wonders, with our own eyes, drawn from a rotten cheft, in a rotten college, for the purpofe of affronting thofe who are willing to believe, that we owe fome of the bleffings we now enjoy, to the honour, fpirit and patriotifm, of fome of our countrymen: of the employer, and of thofe employed in that wife bufinefs, we fhall fay no more than, that thofe who took them out of the cheft, may be well fufpected of having firft put them in.

Thefe ingenious renovations of hiftory, are a fufficient declaration of its inanity: by the reduction of what has been efteemed facts, to probabilities only, we make the whole a romance; but to fet up vague teftimony againft probability, is impudent and wicked. It muft, however, be the deftiny of all relations, to be, in length of time, fubmitted to the opinions and prejudices of thofe, who know nothing of the matter; if it is unfafe to rely on the firft accounts, as impartial, becaufe we fee contradictions, exaggerations and fuppreffions of the Truth, in

Vol. I.   R   the

the authors on both sides the question, it is however difficult to say how the matter is to be set right by a mediator, who, some centuries after, is to find his way to the Truth between these deceivers.

Let us take a view of the history of the unfortunate Mary Queen of Scots, who had the unhappiness to live at the precise period of time, when the almost savage manners of this country and her own, inclined men to reject every thing said of a papist, that was not infamous and reproachful: if we allow that there is much probability in the charges brought against her by her enemies, relative to the death of her husband, and her infatuated connection with Bothwell; by keeping our eye on the vices and atrocious conduct of those who produced and admitted the charges, the suspicions of the blackest treachery, forgeries, and every unworthy attempt to blacken her character, are equally admissible. Such is the state of history, which, as we observed before, is of little consequence, whether it be true or false, or alternately received as such; nay, in the assertion and the contradiction, there is a double portion of matter for reflection, which is the greatest benefit
that

that can result from any reading. We believe that the history of the civil war, by Lord Clarendon, was conscientiously written, but there are strong marks of a narrow, biggoted prejudice, which no writer ever avoided in a like situation: those on the other side, are equally guilty of the same charge.

When Sir Walter Raleigh was confined in the Tower of London, he undertook to write a history of the world. It happened that he was one day disturbed very much, by a wrangling noise under his window; he sent his servant to inquire into it; the man returned with an account, which was contradictory to that which Sir Walter had himself seen and heard; he called up another person, whom he had observed to be near the scene, to clear up the doubts; but after much pains-taking, he could not get at any satisfactory intelligence in the business: upon which he reflected on the nature of his work in hand; here, says he, am I engaged in composing a history of the principal transactions in all the different empires of the world, rejecting some accounts and asserting the veracity of others, and yet I am unable to decide concerning the accounts I have received of a trifling circumstance

that

that paſſed under my window. The reflection was good; but did not prevent the publication of his work.

The ſuppreſſion of what we know to be true, is a miſpriſion of treaſon againſt the majeſty of Truth; and yet we countenance it ſo far in ſociety, that the promulgation of Truth, would, in a variety of circumſtances, be deemed the greateſt breach of good manners, which in its baneful effects would be equivalent to a want of morals.

> Without good breeding Truth is diſapprov'd,
> That only, makes ſuperior ſenſe belov'd.
>
> POPE.

It ought to be no wonder that there is ſo much falſehood in the world, ſince we allow that a free communication of Truth would make us hateful to each other, by deſtroying impoſture, which we tacitly allow to be the chief band of ſocial union.

Truth has the ſame effects on the minds of ſome, that very ſtrong light has upon the organs of viſion: thoſe who think they reſpect Truth the moſt, are not the leaſt liable to reject it; for Truth is not at all times that

that which is true, but that which assumes the appearance of it.

Truth is a deity whom all pretend to reverence and adore; but concerning its nature and attributes, the disputes and distinctions are so various and changeable, that most men behave like atheists, or idolaters; while some few only have capacity and inclination to follow its dictates, with such regard as is due to sacred things.

ESSAY

ESSAY XV.

Of KINGS.

———Pueri ludentes, rex eris, aiunt,
Si recte facies.———

HOR.

The boys at play, cry, you're the King we choose,
If you the sacred trust will not abuse.

IT is observable of the Kings of the most dignified characters in history, that they were not brought up with the prospect of attaining such pre-eminence; and it is a maxim that to be accquainted with obedience is the readiest way to success in the art of governing.

To reign over a people who are to be governed by a system of positive law, is to be only a guarantee of the law, and may be conducted with qualities merely negative;
which

which, neverthelefs, may affure to the fovereign the good will of his people. A King, whofe authority is lefs circumfcribed, fhould ufe fuch means, that his empire may be over the wills of his people rather than their actions; if this is made the principal rule of government, he cannot fail of fuccefs in all his undertakings.

However we fpeak of the unlimited authority of defpotic princes, it appears that there is no one that is not reftrained in fome degree, by certain cuftoms which no human force can wholly abrogate ; cuftoms, that originate from fome phyfical influence of climate generally, which the people refpect and reverence fo much, that their very exiftence feems connected with it. A people deprived of moft of their natural rights, are very ftrenuous to preferve whatever remains to them.

The Czar Peter when he ordered the beards to be cut off, from all thofe who entered the city from the provinces, did not know, or did not regard it, that the cutting off a mans beard in that climate, in Winter, is very diftrefsful, and for which an immediate fuccedaneum can fcarcely be found ; he might have

have contrived something* ornamental to have given them, which would have defended the throat against the severity of the cold, if he had been desirous of appearing the father of his people. In countries where the people are treated with no more respect, they are not subjects. In Russia and Turkey, revolutions are natural consequences, and not violences: if the reign of the present Empress of Russia is an exception to those of her predecessors, it is because the government is changed in her hands; caprice and cruelty, have been replaced by steady conduct and humanity.

It is reckoned no small perfection in a Prince, to know how to employ men according to their respective abilities; but the most sublime art is to make his people what they ought to be, to make them wise and happy, which may be done by attention in framing the laws, and in the execution of them: religion and laws have imposing sounds, but are of little use to the welfare of a country, unless they are applied to the manners of the people.

* The Spanish Ruff was invented to hide the scars in the jugular glands, frequent in that country, from tumours affecting those parts.

Kings are beings very different from other men; their fenfations are of another kind; their exemption from the general lot of hardfhips, in fome degree attending all other fituations, makes them ftrangers to commiferation and fenfibility; the pleafure of friendfhip is exchanged for that of flattery and obfequioufnefs; the nature of their education is calculated to deftroy all natural difpofition, at leaft the effects are the fame as if it were a part of the plan: they begin fo early to live by rules of art, that they are in mafquerade their whole lives; whether their defign be to oblige, or offend, they are equally under the neceffity of employing artifice. There is no other rank in life that can be fo generally defined, becaufe there is no order of men who are trained fo much alike, and have fuch a famenefs of character in fo many refpects.

It is fo much the nature of man to affume power, when the occafion prefents itfelf, that a king is fcarcely blameable if he fubmits to the temptation; the very care of preferving his prerogatives, without any determined intention to increafe them, will naturally produce opportunities; becaufe fome cafes will happen where there is no definition in law, or custom; and when it is left to them to decide, it is easy to see how it must terminate: for Kings seldom consult precedent or reason to control the will of the moment. The watching their prerogatives is without ceasing, whereas what concerns the people, is easily abandoned by their guardians, or found inconvenient to protect; and so neglects accumulate, till the grievances are intolerable, and beget a severe inquiry, or the people submit to the will of the Prince.

Let us for a moment survey the image of a God on earth, if the profanation may be pardoned of using such a comparison: "A "patriot King, A King whose content is "placed in the welfare of his people, who "esteems it his glory to be so circumscri- "bed in his authority, that no wickedness "in his servants can attach his fame in what- "ever they may attempt against the peace "and happiness of the millions, of whom "he is the protector and guardian; from "whom he receives every honour that can "adorn human nature, not as a tribute, but "as a testimony of their unfeigned thanks, "for the pious discharge of his trust." This a King of England may be, and no monarch

on

on earth can pretend to more glorious honours. The defpotic prince, whofe will is the law, philofophically fpeaking, is bound to an obfervance of juftice, and love to his people, if he is emulous of the character of a good man: how contemptible is the prince who is content to fupport an appearance of grandeur, by a conduct that would degrade the meaneft of his fubjects!

The immortal Alfred was a patriot King; and Henry the fourth of France, if he could have been perfuaded that any man in his realm had an exclufive right to the poffeffion of a handfome woman, might have nearly approached to that character.

It is faid, that in one of the royal cabinets on the continent, the names of all the patriot Kings, or Demi-Gods, fince the commencement of hiftory, are written within the circumference of a filver penny, and that there is ftill a vacancy for more.

It may be doubted whether the inventer of the fable of the frogs petitions to Jupiter, for a King, meditated a fatire on the governments of mankind, but it may be fo applied. The Corficans on their petition to Jupiter, received " A log—Theodore. "To other nations

tions have been sent a succession of " storks;" but what is not related of the frogs, the people of the different countries over whom the storks have reigned, have constantly prayed to Jupiter, to preserve King Stork.

ESSAY

ESSAY XVI.

Of LANGUAGE, WIT AND HUMOUR.

Multa renascentur, quæ jam cecidere; cadentque
Quæ nunc sunt in honore vocabula, si volet usus
Quem penes arbitrium est, et jus, et norma loquendi.
Hor.

Some words, like leaves renew'd, burst forth to light,
Fashion dooms others to an endless night,
Her will's the law, no other wrong, or right.

IT is not our intention to inquire concerning the purity of language in composition, or the means of acquiring it, but to make some observations relative to the use and fate of words, of which Language is formed.

Words subsist on no firm basis; their value or signification is liable to be varied by an arbitrary caprice, of which the origin is not often known; obscured and vitiated by time they may become low and obsolete; and if they chance to be used by mean and contemptible writers, or get into vulgar mouths, they, for that reason, are sometimes abandoned, and consigned to oblivion. Words of dignity, at one period, are rejected, sometimes, because they have been applied on some trivial occasion; a recollection of which is unpleasing, and dooms the word never to rise again into consequence.

Pronunciation is a great arbiter; a refinement in that, shall sometimes, in the struggle for admission, consign the word to writers only; it shall in a manner be banished from conversation, for many will dislike the alteration, and the dispute that may attend the use of it. We borrow many words from the French, as the Romans did of the Greeks, to enrich and adorn our language, some of which by degrees get naturalized. Proverbs are the greatest preservers and consecraters of words; a convenient lodging there, secures immortality: for example,

A cold

A cold May, and a Windy,
Makes a full Barn, and a Findy.

It may be that the *Proverb—Weaver was the father of Findy*, and that it has never had other courſe than in this ſenſe, where in the farmers language, it means plump-ear'd, well yielding; like the fly in amber, there's no diſplacing it; if there's a blaſt of wind in May—Findy ſhall be remembered.

Dictionaries are the obituaries of words, and their cemeteries; their laſt hold is there generally; a few indeed ſtruck off that liſt, are found in old favourite authors, like ſome canonized ſaints, with nothing but a name, their virtues all forgotten, to the annoyance of expoſitors and commentators, whoſe anger they defy.

In dictionaries words have their epitaphs ——Quandary,—came over with William the Conqueror—Family name—*Qu'en dirai je?*—paſſed for doubt, ſuſpence of mind— was degraded for keeping low company.

Pleaſe the Pix, whilſt we entertained re-ſpect for the Romiſh church, was like, God willing; we have loſt our reverence for the word,

word, but continue the found, and now some pioufly exclaim, Pleafe the Pigs, I will do fo and fo.

If a man's affairs are perplexed and unfettled, it is faid, they are at fixes and fevens, and every one underftands the implication; the fame words might as well mean, that they are correct and in order, *fi volet ufus ;* in this manner, that which is fix, is fo ftated, and fo of feven, and the other numbers.

In converfation, a negative fometimes implies the affirmative; and a word of affent is ufed, where diffent is underftood.

If a man fays that which is violently againft truth, it may not be decorous to fay fo, and one may even give affent by faying—certainly—furely—meaning certain-lie, fure-lie.

When *ly* is added to the firft adjective, where two are made ufe of, it ftands in the place of *valde*, in Latin, and *bien* in French.

A writer may bring his ftyle to correctnefs and elegance, with only a partial knowledge of a language; of which there are many inftances amongft the writers of Latin, and of our own tongue.

It

It is curious to obferve that the acute Mr. Hume, whofe character and literary merit is worthy of all eftimation, fhould have fpoken fo coldly and unfeelingly of Shakefpear; the truth is, it was not altogether a want of tafte, but that he did not underftand our Language well enough to fee his beauties; and it is but of late that any writers of his country has fhown a relifh for them: the firft we have noted is a Mr. Craufurd; and fince him, two or three others have expreffed a like difpofition, and fome juft obfervations.

It is a very particular circumftance, that the Scottifh nation fhould have been fo long, fuch ftrangers to the Englifh profody, that it is, even now, very rare to find one who is not as eafily diftinguifhed by his tongue, as a German or a Frenchman.

It is without example, we believe, that two people ufing the fame words, fpeak different Languages; for that Language can never be the fame with ours, where the mode of fpeaking, as to time and found, is intirely different. For example:

"A nobleman's widow at Edinburgh, that fpeaks the Englifh Language" *ad aurem*.

English Pronunciation.

A nobleman's wid-ow at Ed-in-borough, that speaks the In-glish Lang-wage.

Scottish.

A nobble-man's weed-er ate Ame-brer, thot spacs the Inglis Long-edge.

And of a like diſtance of character in the tongues, the inſtances are innumerable.

WIT and Humour are of the ſame ſtock with genius, and equally inexplicable. No perſon has yet given a definition of Wit, that precifely meets the approbation of any man of taſte. Dr. Johnſon, whoſe difcernment and ſtrength of mental accompliſhments bade fairly to embrace the whole, like every other attempt, has left a vacancy; which however difficult to fill up, is yet without a clear ſolution of the problem. 'Wit, ſays he, is deſcribed by Mr. Pope, as being "That which has been often thought, but was never before ſo well expreſſed." Which account is certainly erroneous; he depreſſes it below its natural dignity, and reduces it from ſtrength
of

of thought to happiness of language. By a more noble and more adequate conception, " Wit may be considered, as that which is at once natural and new; that which, though not obvious, is upon its first production, acknowledged to be just; and, that which, he that never found it, wonders how he missed."*

Wit is an instinctive faculty of the mind, and has nothing to do with reflection or acquirements, otherwise than, in a well informed mind, the increase of ideas is likely to give it a wider range and more force; but never can create it.

A man may have wit in his own language, and be without the powers of applying it to a foreign one; as is related of one of our English dukes, when in Spain; insomuch, that it has been deemed a kind of folly to expect a translation of wit; yet we venture to say, that Hudibras, the wittiest book in the world, is wonderfully done into French, by a Colonel Townly, formerly in the service of the Empress of Germany; the great difficulty in such a work, is to find a person equal-

* Life of Cowley.

ly well learned in both languages, with a natural fund of Wit and Humour.

Humour is nearly related to Wit, and is equally a particular gift; it often depends on the delivery as to manner; the same words from another person, shall lose half their vigour. Sir John Falstaff observes of Justice Shallow; " I will devise matter enough out of this Shallow to keep Prince Henry in continual laughter the wearing out of six fashions, which is four terms, or two actions; and he shall laugh without intervallums. O, it is much, that a lye with a slight oath, and a jest with a sad brow, will do with a fellow that never had the ache in his shoulders. O, you shall see him laugh, till his face be like a wet cloak ill laid up."

If we attempt to assign the portion of this pointed thought, we call Humour, to each of the three nations forming the British empire; amongst the lower orders of the different people, it will stand, about thus: the Scotch 0; the English 50; the Irish 100. Those who are unacquainted with what is called the blackguard wit of Dublin, have no idea of the sublimity, if we may so say, of some droll ludicrous conceptions, that

that have come from the loweft of mankind in that kingdom: with refpect to men of education, of the different countries, we fhall not prefume to give an opinion.

ESSAY

ESSAY XVII.

Of INGRATITUDE.

Beneficia qui dedisse dicit; petit.

Who boast of benefits bestow'd, contrive
How, by that giving, they themselves may thrive.

TO declaim against Ingratitude is so common, and the vice is of a nature so odious, that every one takes fire at the bare mention of it; but it ought by no means to be admitted so generally and extensively, as a crime frequent and common, which many endeavour to persuade us.

In proportion to the enormity of a crime, it is but just and reasonable that the proof should be more circumstantially correct; and yet

yet this crime, which, perhaps, is almoſt as rare as parricide, is eaſily believed, on the ſlighteſt teſtimony. It is very uſeful and proper, on all occaſions, to conſider the character of the perſon who charges another with any grievous fault; and in the caſe we are ſpeaking of, let due notice be taken, and it will generally be found, that the complaints of want of gratitude, are in proportion to the want of generoſity in the perſon who exhibits them: for to do an act, where generoſity is the baſis, there can be no ingratitude follow. To relieve the wants of a perſon in diſtreſs, from the pure deſire of doing good to a fellow-creature, is clear of all obligation from the perſon aſſiſted; otherwiſe it is to barter that which one ſeems to give, for the proſpect of receiving ſomething as good, or better, in diſcharge of the favour.

It is as impoſſible to conceive, that any perſon ſhould reſolve to do evil in return for ſome benefit; as that any guilt was ever incurred, for the purpoſe of bringing down the vengeance of the deity upon the head of the tranſgreſſor: theſe caſes are nearly parallel; for in both, there is that unaccountable perverſion of mind, we call madneſs.

Many excuse themselves from a readiness to assist the distressed, because, say they, one meets with nothing but Ingratitude from the poor. The generous person considers those in adversity, as poor in every thing. The mind of a distressed man is inactive and debilitated with his body, suffering for want of sustenance: a remissness of attention may therefore be expected. Some are not content if the manner of receiving their bounty, is not to their mind; forgetting, that really and truly to give, is, to resolve to put another in the free and full possession of whatever is bestowed. But what more can be expected in acknowledgement of small favours, than obsequiousness? which is in its nature so trifling and ridiculous, that no one will dare to acknowledge himself so mean, as to wish to exact it.

Every person who is in the habit of relieving the distresses of his fellow creatures, will necessarily meet with some, who from the nature of their disposition, entertain a more expressive sense of favours than others; but the appearance of it requires but little art, and is often practised in expectation of further favour from those, who are known to be pleased with such acknowledgements.

How

How many bestow that, which to the world may have the appearance of generosity, and is to the receiver the source of misery and discontent. How often does pride, lust, and self-interest assume the habit of charity, and a right to load the object of their supposed favour, with the crime of Ingratitude, if they are disappointed in their projects ! no one can know the motives with which any act is done in the way of charity, but the least claim to a return, annihilates every pretence to merit in those, who know so little how to give.

A person may lend money to another, to assist him in his business, or concerns ; a like favour may be expected from the person borrowing, and yet a refusal may not be Ingratitude. Money may be lent where there was no risk to the lender; but if he expects the like assistance, when he may be in a situation which disables him from returning the money, it must be allowed, that here is not a parity of circumstances ; for what was only a civility in one, would in the other be the highest generosity.

We cannot help observing, that there is a very respectable order of men in society, who are often charged with Ingratitude, from their very peculiar situation, more than from any other cause; what they have must be given, and the donor is too often liable to overrate the nature of the present. The higher the spirit and sensibility of the person receiving a favour, the more delicate and liberal should be the manner of bestowing; and above all in what we advert to, from the nature of the thing given, and received.

They who insist upon the perverseness of human nature, and have a pleasure in attributing every sinister motive to mankind, pretend that men are naturally ungrateful. No man is, to speak philosophically, naturally good or bad. Self-interest is too apt to mislead such as deliver themselves up to its guidance; and in this case, where it is to a man's profit and honour, as in every other, to behave with justice and propriety, the mind may sometimes deviate.

The recompence for giving, is in the contemplation of the motive in one's own mind; and if it is done from the pure desire of diffusing happiness, the person feels himself exalted into the highest order of human beings.

The fountain yields its fpontaneous refreſhments to all that apply, and finds no dimunition from its largeſſes: ſo it is with the truly generous and charitably difpofed mind.

ESSAY XVIII.

Of REVERIES, or BUILDING CASTLES IN THE AIR.

Animum nunc huc celerem, tunc dividit illuc,
In partesque rapit varias, perque omnia versat.
                                    VIRG.

A thousand ways his ready mind divides,
And shifts the scene as his gay Fancy guides.

IF there are men who have been so occupied, and have had such full success in the conduct of their affairs, as never to have wandered in the regions of Fancy, we know not whether to congratulate or pity them; for we presume not to affront content in mere mortal man, in whatever shape, or by whatsoever fair means it may be procured.

We

We fometimes find amongſt our acquaintance one who defpifes fuch employment, as unworthy to intrude itfelf into the mind of a man, who has the power of beſtowing his reflection on things, which come nearer to the means of effecting folid and permament benefits, as he terms them. He who regards all reflection as loſt time which is not directed to fome felfiſh purpofe of getting money, if he has been fortunate in his fpeculations, is apt to fwell with pride on that account, and to be difguſted with all other, as ſhort of true wifdom.

The French call our amuſement, " *a faire des Chateaux en Eſpagne :* " A Frenchman's building a caſtle in Spain, or an Engliſhman to conſtruct one in the air, may be deemed labours of the fame kind. The antiquity of this airy mafonry, is certainly equal with that of free-mafonry; the arcana of which fcience, has always been depofited with the moſt wife, as may be difcovered in their liſts of patrons, or grand maſters, from Tubal Cain to the prefent times. We alfo reckon the wifeſt among the Jews, as an adept in our fcience of caſtle-building in the air; as may be gathered from the *Solomoniana.*

niana. Among the Gentiles, we have Plato, Ariftotle, and every philofopher before or fince of any note; and for good chriftians and true followers of Mahomet, we claim them all of every fect.

In the beft fyftem of education, one great object is recommended above all others: "That we feek for content in our own minds." All the rules of the higheft authority agree in the cenfure of attachment to thofe things which are vulgarly called fubftantial, fuch as may be purchafed with riches, and are the objects of fenfuality; or if any thing of that fort is allowed, to the animal part, by way of regale, it is always granted under terms which prefcribe the moft temperate ufe, left too clofe an attention in the purfuit, fhould interfere with the fublime occupations of the mind.

We fhall find, however, that the heights of philofophy, are fometimes reached by one, we never fufpected of fuch acquirements; and by a nearer road than the the moft fubtle of our preceptors have marked out. For inftance: The good creature who can lean over a bridge, watching the *Labitur et Labetur,* 'till his dinner is ready, perhaps for two hours;

hours; if curiofity fhould inquire after the nature of his amufement, he anfwers without refervation, " That he was thinking of nothing at all."

They who are accuftomed to compare extremes, know how nearly things, the moft oppofite in their natures, refemble each other: if we incline to place the paffive philofopher we have defcribed, befide our aerial architect, it is from a fincere love of juftice, and a deference to all the harmlefs of the human kind; but we are far from admitting him to march *pari paſſu*.

If the practice of our delectable paftime is oftentimes the refource of the unfortunate, whom accident or ill fuccefs, has driven from the enjoyment of thofe more in requeft with the gay and thoughtlefs, yet as it is frequently the lot of fome amongft the moft deferving, our refpect for it, ought not to be leffened on that account; and it fhould be remembered that we have it in charge amongft our earlieft maxims, that we can never arrive at a proper relifh for the higher pleafures, which are to be the refult of our mental labours, whilft we have the incumbrance of goods and chattels.

When

When house and land is gone and spent,
Then learning is most excellent.

The French too have a maxim of the same colour.

Qui terre a,
Guerre a. *

The source of happiness is neither entirely in the object desired, nor in the mind which is possessed of it; there must be that necessary concurrence, the relation between them, to produce this delicious sensation.

Happiness depends so much upon opinion, that our art cannot reasonably be charged with folly and delusion, more than any other pursuit in quest of pleasure. He who denies that he has not received a fuller enjoyment in the contemplation of some future pleasure, than he experienced in the fruition, has not attained the highest felicity that our nature is capable of. All philosophers agree that the imagination ornaments, in the greatest degree, the objects of our attainments, but quits us in the possession; is it a question then,

* He who has land,
Has strife at hand.

which is the substantial? what is the employment of the young and the voluptuous, but the illusion of imaginary pleasures?

Every one is acquainted with the story of a man at Athens, who had the art to make himself the owner, in idea, of all the vessels that arrived at the port ; till at length, some wise, meddling friend, undertook to oust him, of what he termed, " his imaginary possessions:" but it was soon seen how substantial they were, for the poor man never held up his head after the loss. Many are ready enough to pronounce on the case of this Athenian, that he was insane; but we who are not to be imposed upon by technical terms, and aware of the small difference there is, between madness in such proper bounds, and the most deliberate and refined wisdom and wit, are not so free to determine the matter; more especially, as some, who have been esteemed very acute observers, have in our opinion been grosly misled in such decisions.

There are no men better acquainted with madness, than the best poets : Mr. Pope assures us, that the division or partition between wit and madness, is very thin; from whence we may suppose, that they resemble each other so much, that one is often passed upon us for the other: how common is the observation from a person who has just visited bedlam, speaking of a particular person there, that, except on such a subject, he was like any other reasonable man? which in the Shandean style, is no more than being hobby-horsical, and is so generally seen out of bedlam, as not to excite admiration, beyond fox-hunting, and some other amusements.

It has been thrown out by some wit, that there are many appearances to countenance the opinion, " that all the madmen which might have made a portion of the inhabitants in the other planets, are constantly sent here." He probably supposed, that the quantity of morbific matter of that kind, which a man may safely carry about him with us, might in the planet Mercury turn to rage and biting; and in Saturn and the Georgium Sidus, from their extreme distance from the Sun, it might be attended with such imbecility of mind and body, as to require slavering-bibs; whereas in our midway station, it seems to be in its proper region, and is passed off in a manner unnoticed, or at least without causing much alarm. However wide of the truth the guefs may be, with refpect to the other planets, it may be afferted, that we, in calling ourfelves reafonable creatures, in contra-diftinction to other animals, which are each known by their peculiarly confiftent mode of acting, make ufe of a loofe and arbitrary definition, of which we could give a variety of inftances.

We think lightly of a general who will rifk nothing againft the reafonable appearances of not being fuccefsful ; we are apt to fay he fhould have tried every thing, and in that we are juft enough to confefs, that madnefs, or a conduct againft reafon is often better than reafon itfelf. Of war, we fhall only obferve, that, philofophically fpeaking, the bufinefs of knocking each other on the head, fhould not take place, till our globe were fo fully inhabited that the earth and fea could not furnifh fubfiftence for all : if this argument is good for nothing elfe, the pleafure we find in deftroying our fellow creatures in war, will at leaft ferve to diftinguifh us from the other orders of animals, equally with what is called reafon.

Romance writing, which is an humble imitation of our aerial employment, was probably

bably invented for the use of those who are scanty in ideal materials, or want the ingenuity to range them in proper order. When these compositions have the best effects that can reasonably be expected, by their display of the pleasures attending heroic and amiable deportment, they persuade the reader, if he has any taste for such qualities, to assume, at least for a time, something more exalted than his ordinary behaviour: but that these impressions are lasting, in many minds, we cannot affirm.

We have noticed this effect to be very general, that any person whose conduct challenges a more than common esteem, the acknowledgement where it cannot decently be refused, is accompanied with this observation, " that the person spoken of is very romantic," or in other words, much beyond what we ever expect to attain; for that is the application which without exception, belongs to this inuendo.

What may we not expect to be said of one who pretends, that for want of opportunity to show his good disposition in action, frequently passes his leisure, in bringing home to his feelings, all those pleasures which the reality

reality could excite, by the trick of mere fancy! That at one time he is a generous magistrate, receiving respect from the province where he resides; at another time, he is a brave citizen, fighting in the defence of liberty; or raising his views still higher, he deplores the miseries of despotism, and emulous of the immortal Alfred, he is a patriot king.

For his more ordinary pastimes, he takes possession of some estate near him, invited by the beauty of its situation, and the neglect of the owner; walks over the fields, and names them to his mind, prunes the eglantine and woodbine, and receives a fuller satisfaction from his intimacy with their natural beauties, than the legal possessor derives from the revenue of them.

He risks nothing in his enjoyments; he usurps nothing to the annoyance of any one, in mind, body or estate; and how uncommon foever such amusement may be, as different in those respects from the pursuits of most other men; the novelty of it, should in justice secure him from reproach.

We shall take no offence at being called flighty

flighty, yet we could point out many who are reputed grave and sober-minded, whom we neither envy nor despise, that think themselves never better employed, than when they carry their speculations much beyond our attempts.

Of the HUMAN MIND.

OF all the operations of nature, her work of the Human Mind is the most variable. Its changes are as frequent with the wise, as the unlearned: this is well enough understood amongst men, and if it were as well remembered, would be the death of many prejudices that set us at variance. No two men can think alike on every subject, and so continue; for every man is constantly varying from himself: most men, indeed, affect an uniformity of character, to prevent the notoriety of their deviations and though it may make most of them invisible, it does not prevent them. The greatest miser will sometimes

sometimes give a sum of money, beyond what the most habitually generous would bestow.

It is a maxim with the Turks, that no man should be surprized if another changes his mind; they say wisely enough, every one but a fool will do so; and we acknowledge no less, when we call a man an obstinate blockhead.

What is the acquirement of understanding, but the changing a wrong opinion for one that is right! the persisting in old notions, generally proceeds from a want of discernment, rather than from a conviction of their rectitude.

Those who read and reflect much, will find, that from twenty years of age to sixty, they have varied in their opinions of every thing serious and trifling: habits, maxims concerning health, religion, and in short, all concerns whatever, all change by a gradual progression, without whim, or violence put upon their understanding. These things happen to many who never observe it: even morals, in the course of time, will take another cast, if not strictly watched. The respect

spect paid to ill-acquired riches, and the want of it to those who have none, help, with other observations, to warp the mind. Old men are generally less nice than in their youth; to them the pronoun possessive *meum*, is really a magnet.

ESSAY XIX.

Of PRUDENCE AND FORTUNE.

Nullum numen habes*, si sit prudentia: sed te
Nos facimus, Fortuna, deam, cæloque locamus.
JUVENAL.

Fools worship Fortune, place her in the skies,
Prudence is god, and goddess to the wise.

PRUDENCE, or practical wisdom, is the exertion of our understanding, to foresee and prevent all adventitious circumstances, from disposing events contrary to our intentions, or rather the appearance of it; for it may be doubted if any person did ever combine so much address and management,

---

* Voltaire and some others, *abest*.

as to secure a certainty respecting things out of his own power, however the success might favour the appearance.

Fortune, if not actually at war with Prudence, does however often assert her superiority very arbitrarily: amongst the Romans, whose superstition increased their mythology beyond all reasonable bounds, both were worshipped as goddesses, and had their temples and votaries. Fortune seems to have had most adorers; for she had all the unwise: some who had been the objects of her favour, had yet the presumption to attribute it to Prudence, because with that goddess they could share the glory; it being easy to pass off her inspirations, for their own suggestions. If Prudence is dwindled into human wisdom, Fortune is now neither worshipped, nor honoured with any confidence; and when they had the most influence, they were both generally treated with ingratitude, by those whom they had favoured.

Timoleon, who was a successful general, modestly attributed the whole of his good fortune to the Gods, or Fortune; reserving nothing to be ascribed to his own Prudence. Sylla, who had received stronger marks of favour,

favour, both in his tyranny and retreat from business, assumed nothing to himself; but he was suspected of artifice, in this affectation of humility. So presumptuous is the human conceit, that we cannot pardon the want of arrogance in another; if we implore divine assistance, and it is granted, we challenge a part of the success to ourselves without shame: the ancients were particularly in dread of the goddess Nemesis, who was a great chastiser of insolence arising from success; much reverse of Fortune, was attributed to her.

Cardinal Richlieu, who was a great intriguer, and used all sorts of means to compass his ends, attributed all his successes to his own discernment: he admitted of nothing as unfortunate, but where imprudence had governed. In one sense it is true, that something may be discovered in every unfortunate event under human government, where the administration of other conduct would have changed the circumstances; but this is frivolous, for that something may be so extraneous, as could never have occurred to any foresight,

We all acknowledge an invisible and arbitrary

bitrary interference, we call good and bad luck, which wait on most men, and decide upon their welfare through life; on some is bestowed success at games of chance, others are prosperous in all they undertake; all avenues to success lie open before them. In 1774 there was at Paris a Dantzick banker, who had been concerned in the English state lottery, in two tickets only, at different times; in one, the half only belonged to him, the other wholly; they were both 20000l.

Human Prudence is by some so undervalued, that they proverbially say, Fools have Fortune. The ancients, had their *audaces fortuna juvat**. Some men are so confident of success, that they conduct their affairs as if Fortune was their slave. Cesar, who had all the advantages that attend the greatest Prudence, had still a greater confidence in his good fortune; and thought nothing so proper to rouze the sinking courage of his boatman, in a frightful storm, as to say him, "Fear nothing, you carry Cesar and his Fortune:" It was necessary to do what he did; death, or a disappointment in his enterprize, were equal. In the attempt to infuse this con-

* The rash are fortune's favourites.

fidence

fidence into the breaſt of another, his behaviour was of the moſt exalted heroiſm; and yet we muſt confeſs, that the briliancy of the action is in the ſucceſs: if he had been drowned, what might not have been ſaid of his conduct! Lord Bacon thinks that Ceſar had only done half if he had ſaid, " you carry Ceſar and his virtues:" we more readily conſign the management of a thing, to a fortunate man, than to one merely virtuous.

On the other hand, ſome are ſo unfortunate that the relation of their diſaſters reſembles a romance; to recapitulate the examples that come within our own obſervation, which belong to good and ill Fortune, would be almoſt endleſs. None will argue in favour of putting Prudence aſide, though many of good judgement may be found, who confeſs that their beſt conceived meaſures have had a worſe iſſue than doing nothing: from whence came the *proverb, melius infelici nihil agere.**

It was an eſtabliſhed maxim with the ancients, that induſtry and human forecaſt were of little avail, againſt the concurrence of un-

* It is better for the unfortunate to do nothing.

foreſeen

foreseen accidents, *sunt in iis quidem virtutis opera magna, sed majora fortunæ.*† Pliny says this, and Quintus Curtius much the same respecting Alexander; and of all military glory, Cornelius Nepos affirms the greater part to belong to Fortune: Cicero, Livy and Diodorus Siculus, say, that we are to judge of men, not by their success, which is in the hands of Fortune, but by the means they had taken to succeed. If the opinion of a prince is of more consequence, let us listen to Philip king of Macedon, who being asked why he had not preserved the kingdom, as his father had left it, answered, "do not wonder; though my father left me his other good things, he did not leave me his good Fortune, by which he acquired them."

Some have argued, that our holy religion has demolished the temples and idols of Fortune, and so it may; but if providence refuses those things we wish for as necessary to our comfort, and which we labour incessantly to acquire; when we see them take a course apparently in opposition to human reasoning, if we believe that they are with-held for our good, we do our duty

† There are in those things, indeed, great efforts of valour, but greater of Fortune.

by

by submitting with a chearful resignation; but we must confess that the solution of the problem is deferred.

Let us make an abstract of Monsieur Bayle's arguments, who was an eminent logical gladiator:

1. The notions of the ancients, though they painted Fortune blind, were not that she made no distinctions in her distributions, but, as we say of a Prince who may be too liberal, that he follows rather the impulse of the moment, than the dictates of reason and justice: they thought the sovereign power possessed by different deities, attributing to them the imperfections of our nature, and particularly to Fortune, the highest degree of caprice; which made them the more solicitous to secure her favour. The philosophers who acknowledged the unity of the Godhead, called him, Fortune; they did not accuse the deity of injustice, but said his ways were not our ways.

2. Under the Gospel, we bestow on earthly things all the defects that the Pagans attributed to Fortune, as a divinity; the possession of worldly goods, we say, is no mark

mark of merit in the poffeffor; that they are perifhable, and deceive thofe who put their truft in them.

3. They did not deny that there were fortunate men, and unlucky ones, in commerce, play, fuccefs at court, and in military feats particularly; but in all they fay concerning Cefar, Timoleon, Sylla and Alexander, there is nothing, but what is exactly conformable to maxims of a later date.

4. It is falfe to fay that good or ill Fortune depends on Prudence, or the want of it; the winner at play is not always the beft player. The moft experienced gamefters quit play when Fortune declares againft them, and double their ftakes if they can, when fhe appears to encourage them. It is the fame in induftry, and all other concerns; there is an imperceptible fomething that opens the courfe, or fhuts the road to fuccefs.

5. Princes generally judge by the fuccefs of thofe they employ, concerning their defert: the conqueror, and vanquifhed are differently received, however the merits of their caution and Prudence may be. A fortunate

tunate rashness, you say, was Prudence, since the event has shown that the measure was adapted to the purpose. The answer to which is, that rashness is not governed by rule and proportion; therefore, to chance, and not to Prudence, the success belongs. It is not from imprudence that we do not discover the accidents hidden from human foresight: in a variety of business, how shall a man see what malice, lies, and jealousies may effect, that strike without warning?

6. Since no man is the principal cause of his good or ill fortune, the difficulty is to know what that Fortune is, which regulates the success of some, and persecutes others, without regard to their desert, or the measures they take. If you say providence is the disposer of all events, you provoke a world of argument against you; they will not easily allow that it can follow from general laws, that some should be always fortunate, and others unlucky.

7. The last reflection, is, that men murmur excessively against Fortune, and often throw their imprudence upon her interference; though he allows that she often deprives a man of his natural powers to assist himself;

as in the case of Pompey, at the battle of Pharsalia; where Fortune declaring for Cesar, Pompey did nothing becoming his former prudence, valour, or generalship.*

By this time it may be easily seen, that there is no conducting any one to evidence and demonstration on this subject; but nothing can be more clear, than that providence, or the want of it, does not decide on good or ill success.

No man plays without superstition; what pocket pieces to mark with, turning of chairs and a hundred other fooleries are practised, openly, to engage Fortune; to say nothing of orisons, and other silent conceits. Very few engage in the state lottery without prepossession in favour of numbers; perhaps no man likes the number of the last year's great prize, yet the chance is absolutely no greater against that number this year, than it was before.

Our chief content depends on the moderation of our expectations; we should look at mediocrity as the surest means of producing content, and believe that those things which

* Fol. Amsterdam edit. vol. 4. p. 373.

are refused us, have something in their acquisition, however imperceptible it may be, that would not suit us; and to be assured that the great dispenser of all things, loves justice and mercy, and will remunerate.

Prudence, in the common acceptation of the word, is a conduct guided by those mean, sordid principles, which a sincere love of self excites, void of all accommodation to others which may call upon our purse, or prevent our own acquisitions; it is generally glossed over with an obliging behaviour, that is geometrically squared, so as to give no offence, and keep off all very distinguished attachment, that might expose our safety and well doing to jeopardy.

The real Prudence is a combination of all the virtues that can belong to our nature; the display of which, always creates a respect, little short of adoration, wherever it is found; but is so far from insuring an increase of fortune, that it may perhaps sometimes be an impediment.

We have seen how difficult it is to chain down Fortune, or success in life: the situation from which most may be expected, has generally

generally the most unfavorable appearance; that is to say, that, in which all depends on ourselves, clear of all foreign or external expectations of assistance.

A small fortune, or something above that, if seconded by a profession, is generally a seduction from strenuous application; and the dependance upon it, is attended with indolence and idleness, that prevent all great acquirements. A large fortune easily persuades the owner, that carelesness and neglect may be repaired by future care and discretion, till the confirmed habit brings on ruin.

The young man, who has no expectations but from his own behaviour, seeing constantly that the least deviation from honour and probity, will be followed by debt and disgrace, will acquire the habit of living on his income; which by his diligence, will be sure to mend: thus success is in a manner forced upon him, by having nothing to impede his industry, which will certainly carry him forward to lasting content.

ESSAY XX.

Of SENSIBILITY AND BENEVOLENCE.

Non ignara mali, miseris succurrere disco.
                                    VIRG.

Touch'd by misfortune's heavy hand, I know,
What pleasure 'tis to ease another's woe.

NEVER were fine feelings in greater estimation, nor more generally adopted, than in our time; for so far from their being confined to the natural delicacy of the softer sex, as more congenial with their frame and texture, we hear of them from all quarters. Our public assemblies, for the dispatch of the national business, are even subject to their influence. The ins and outs

complain

complain, at different times, of outrages committed againſt their feelings, by the oppoſite party. If politicians do really undergo ſuch oppreſſions, we are forced to confeſs that we are at a loſs to account for it. If we incline to the belief of the patriots being ſometimes in earneſt, which as they are always out of place are certainly the moſt irritable, we cannot however allow the ſame indulgence to thoſe who are in; but as it is at beſt a technical term, which originated in the boarding ſchool or at the toilette table, we may conſider it as a redundancy in our language, very uſeleſs to gentlemen who ſpeak *ore rotundo*. Not to have fine feelings, Mrs. Slipſlop would ſay, is to be a Notmantot, and eat raw fleſh.

The deſire of exalting our character by the affectation of an extraordinary regard for the welfare of our fellow creatures, is a deceit which ſprings from unworthy motives; but to arrogate to ourſelves ſomething of this ſort, as is frequently practiſed at the expence of thoſe who are preſent, is more than uncivil, and borders on vice.

If we examine the true cauſe of a more than common kindneſs of diſpoſition, it
                                              muſt

muſt ariſe, either from ſome happy combination in our natural conſtitution, from habits impreſſed by thoſe to whom we are indebted for their care and example at an early time, or it is the reſult of a well determined principle to yield every aſſiſtance to the human kind, from a nice obſervation of the neceſſity there is for the exertion of our benevolence to all mankind; but the mediation from all, or either of theſe cauſes, is modeſt and unaſſuming. The truly generous perſon feels all the pleaſure, that the act of relieving another can afford, without looking for admiration, or charging any perſon with want of kindneſs; the occaſion preſents itſelf, and he does that, which he readily concludes many others would have done under like circumſtances.

We may allow that ſenſibility or quickneſs of perception, appears to be more the portion of the fair ſex than the other, as appertaining to their conſtitutional make; from whence many women are apt to believe that tenderneſs of diſpoſition belongs to them excluſively. If we duly examine the matter, it will, perhaps, be found to be no inherent quality ariſing from conſtitution; for we often

ten see inftances in perfons from whom we might expect a greater fenfibility for others; a fympathy on account of their own fufferings from ficknefs, or a peculiar delicacy of make, in whom this quality is counteracted by that very caufe; or in other words, when we wifh to excite commiferation towards ourfelves, we are generally lefs fufceptible of beftowing it on others; fome are fo complaifant to themfelves, as to take merit from beftowing a " God blefs you " on a perfon in diftrefs: fuch a barren difplay of difcharging the duties of human life, may pafs for a civility, but is far enough from an act of benevolence, where there is a power of doing fomething more fubftantial.

Why are not all thofe who voluntarily give themfelves up to tendernefs in a feigned cafe of diftrefs, as at a play, to weep for Hecuba, equally affected by a fcence of real woe? it is becaufe the emotions are independent of any uneafinefs on their own account; the tone of voice and gefture of the actor, the fpectators and the complacency of temper in which we go to fee a tragedy, all affift in drawing tears from us; and fome flatter themfelves fo far as to think, that they exhibit

bit full testimony of their being easily impressed with benevolent feelings, at the sight of distress; whereas to perform that which the necessities of an unfortunate person might require, would call for activity, consolation and our purse; troubles that would rouze our indolence, and try our merit, which we are glad to be exempt from.

The bloody Sylla might weep at the recital of the misfortunes of Andromache or Priam, although he could, without emotion, hear the cries of those whom his sanguinary proscriptions had doomed to death.

No one pities that in another, generally speaking, which he feels himself in no danger of suffering. Kings rarely estimate themselves as a portion of mankind, and have therefore been seldom seen to show a superabundant anxiety for their subjects. A rich man cares not for the poor, because he is in no dread of that situation; poverty combined with sickness may make him susceptible, because he is liable to the latter: this is no censure, nor urged as a necessary consequence, but it is a bias that the frailty of our nature is but too apt to take. It will however be found upon observation, that the poor

poor are very unfeeling for each other, from another cause; they are senfible of the danger of becoming objects of commiseration, or perhaps are so, but it does not produce pity for their fellows; they are affected, as if they were candidates for the fame thing, and are actuated by that jealousy which such a situation excites, and they are often dejected when relief is administered to another.

Pity is one of the first senfations of the human heart; our early wants incline us to it: but it is unequally bestowed in every person; the modifications are different, and belong to the character of every individual: some are moved by cries and tears, others deaf to them, yield to the fight of blood, and yet feel nothing from saying that to another, which will be remembered in anguish during life.

Some men pride themselves in being inflexible; they can be just they say, but despife clemency and humanity, as weaknesses. What is generofity, humanity, clemency and even juftice, but an application of pity to the diftressed, to the culpable, and to the human kind in general? Friendship is but the constant

SENSIBILITY and BENEVOLENCE.

ftant production of pity, directed to a particular object, or the exertion of our endeavours that fuch a perfon may have no wants, and be happy. It feems a peculiar kind of misfortune in our natural conformation, that we fhould be able to feel, with fome exactnefs, the condition of a perfon in diftrefs; but have no power to affimilate ourfelves to thofe, who are more happy than we are; but it is not without its ufe; for whoever will reflect on this, can never want an incitement to Benevolence.

In the general provifion for the poor in this country, a man may appear to himfelf without reproach, in refufing to give any to beggars; but notwithftanding what the laws have done, there is a want of fomething in the execution of them, that leaves many in a deplorable fituation. But without refting on this, thofe who have the means of affiftance, know, that the poor are their brethren, and that without hardening their hearts, they cannot with-hold the pittance that is afked.

The greateft part are vagabonds,—we allow it; but we are too well acquainted with the evils of life, not to know, that there are

many

many circumstances, which may unavoidably reduce an honest man to such a state: sometimes even nice sensibility and a laudable pride, may drive him from those, who had been accustomed to consider him with respect; and how can we tell but that this unknown, who in the name of God asks for a morsel of bread, may be this honest man, ready to perish through misery, and that our refusal may drive him to despair.

A trifle, though no real succour, is however a consolation, is a courtesy, and a testimony that we take a part in their misery: whatever we may think of these unfortunate wretches, we owe something to ourselves, to our ability from what Providence has put into our hands, to our rank in life, and to the example we may be to others.

We ought not to encourage any to be beggars, but when they are so, a small assistance to their wants, may preserve them from being thieves: the giving a trifle, may have this two-fold good effect, it may save oneself from the reproach of having committed a fault, and the life of the person, who implores our aid: for no one can tell how

how near the poor person may be to extremity, from the operation of the passions, or the want of bodily refreshment. It may be said, that the generous are often imposed upon by an affected appearance of distress, by mere acting; we allow it, yet those who have often thought a crown well bestowed on a Garrick, a Pritchard and a Clive, will not think much of a few pence to an under-actor.

Pity is sometimes a weakness arising from a natural defect in the constitution, and is then generally exhausted in words and grimace; which, as we observed before, sometimes imposes so far on persons thus constited, as to persuade them that they are acting above human nature, when they display their tenderness alike to cats, dogs, monkies, and the human race; they have a tear for all, as it may be required; but if such persons would take the pains to examine themselves, they might discover, that they are of a sniveling constitution, and that the tears they so liberally bestow, are really an accommodation to themselves, and of no use to any other creature.

There are many persons, whose compassion is

is unbounded without any mixture of weakness, not only to their fellow creatures, but to every part of animated nature, upon the principles of pure Benevolence; and to such the sight of distress, spontaneously creates endeavours to relieve it, which are attended with the highest gratification, that the mind is susceptible of: to relieve the distresses of the poor and wretched is the only act, by which we can pretend to imitate divine goodness.

A

LETTER

ON

EDUCATION.

LETTER

ON

EDUCATION.

Dear Sir,

THE contrariety of argument to be met with in the different systems proposed for the Education of youth, evinces the difficulties which belong to the subject; for without saying any thing of the mode of instruction, some will have it administered in great schools only, whilst others contend for such as receive a small number. I shall, therefore, communicate to you some observations I have made, which you will perceive are not intended to support either opinion, or recommended as applicable to a general use.

Mr. Locke, in his "Thoughts concerning Education," propofes nothing more than to make his pupil an healthy and virtuous gentleman. I fay, nothing more; becaufe in the univerfal practice of all great fchools, they certainly intend nothing lefs than that. Whilft he is content to give rules for the forming an happy and virtuous member of fociety, the grammarians hold out the flattering hopes of fupplying the nation with great choice of lord chancellors, arch-bifhops, and judges.

They who argue in favour of great fchools, dwell much on the fharpnefs that may be acquired there; but very wifely fay nothing of manners and morals. They reckon much upon the future benefits from connections they will form with the young nobility; which, it muft be allowed, may be ufeful in the metropolis, to a man of Weftminfter-hall, a phyfician, or church-man, provided he is of eminence enough in his profeffion to do without them. There is no denying that fome men have profited by fuch accidents, and fome have gotten the greateft prize in the ftate lottery. Such pleafing reveries fuit very well with the wifdom of thofe parents, who will abate nothing of riches or honours to their darling reprefentatives.

I have feen many inftances where the defire of being particularly noticed, by thofe of a very fuperior rank, has been attended with a fevere difappointment, or a dear earned compenfation; and this is fo common, that it may be deemed a natural confequence.

The pompous difplay that is made of the methods of teaching Latin and Greek, by a difcipline full of heart-breaking mifery to children of a delicate frame, and which is of little ufe to the robuft who can mufter refolution to meet it, is matter of laughter to thofe who have paffed through it. One boy in twenty has the good fortune to difcharge his mind and memory of all repetition, fyntax, and profody, that may be put to him, without knowing more of the matter than thofe who had done their beft, had funk under the burden and were punifhed.

I fhall not enlarge upon the vicious and idle habits which are, in a manner, inculcated in the firft-rate fchools; to which a right reveverend prelate belonging to one of the univerfities, has imputed the fmall gains now acquired there: the silent admonitions of old college rules, or the gravity of a proctor, make slight impressions on the minds of those who have been initiated in the orgies of Covent-Garden.

Schools are very convenient and necessary to parents, whose professions in life put it out of their power to superintend the Education of their children; to such whose love of pleasure inclines them to consider their offspring as a drain to their purse; and to those who cannot support the expence of a private tutor.

The man who has well reflected on his duty as a father, will admit nothing of small concern to interfere with one of so much weight as the Education of his children. The too general practice of sending infants from home to be nursed, where the parents can bear the charge attending its being done under their own eyes, and afterwards continuing the banishment by packing them off to schools, may shield such parents from censure, but no argument can be produced to excuse the cruelty and injustice of the measure.

They

They who have not had what is called a good Education, and have been fortunate in their enterprizes, are ever ready to believe that, with such an advantage, they might have compassed much greater things, and conclude that every avenue to success is secured to their children, if masters and teachers of all kinds are provided. They go to work as if good sense and genius were marketable, and that the different sciences might be stuffed into the cranium, as one would pack a portmanteau; whilst those who have received the advantages that belong to the customary modes of Education, if they happen to have a turn for study and the attainment of knowledge, can readily estimate the value of what may justly be placed to the account of seven years toiling at the unintelligible jargon of Pædagogues.

Rousseau says, that if a boy was taught nothing till he was twelve years of age, he would have as much understanding at fifteen, as if the greatest pains had been taken to instruct him from the earliest age; and insists, with every appearance of truth, that his mind would be the stronger. But as it is scarcely possible to keep down inquiry concerning a variety of objects that would excite it, even

in

in the moſt retired ſituation, his aſſertion goes chiefly to this, That the anſwering their queſtions in the moſt plain and ſimple method, which is the ſloweſt mode of inſtruction, is all the information that children are capable of receiving: what is got in this manner is their own, and not to be effaced like the faint impreſſions made on their minds by what they do not comprehend, or wiſh not to be acquainted with.

He inſiſts much on the early part of Education being of the greateſt conſequence, and would have this committed to the female part of the family, as the propereſt guardians of the infant ſtate; which he wiſhes alſo to be prolonged. The mildneſs of diſpoſition in women, the dependance which many mothers, if they become widows, muſt have on their ſons, their being conſtantly at hand to give them due attendance; all theſe things intereſt them more in the ſucceſs of their endeavours, than can be expected from a father.

How many will be ready to thunder out their anathemas againſt ſuch folly, as committing boys to the care of their mothers, who will certainly ſpoil them! If a Mother ruins her child's diſpoſition, by an ill-judged indulgence,

indulgence, in that fhe is certainly to blame. If a mother is defirous that her child fhould be happy, in that fhe is reafonable; and if fhe miftakes the means, fhe may be fet right: but are there not forty children who receive irreparable damage from the ambition, tyranny, avarice, negligence, foolifh forefight, and brutal infenfibility of fathers, to one who is hurt by the extreme tendernefs of a mother?

No man in his fenfes will difpute for the preference between a father or mother, where both are equally alike improper for the charge; but *cæteris paribus*, the mother is the beft: a woman of good fenfe, is to be preferred to a fenfible man. Thofe who affect to defpife female guardians, may not know, that the Romans, in the zenith of their glory, committed the care of their fons to the women of the houfhold, till they were eight years of age.

There are two miftakes in particular, that parents are liable to; an extreme readinefs to publifh any errors they difcover in their child's conduct, and to fhow a petulant anxiety at its not taking learning, as they call it, fo quick as they wifh. For the firft,

if

if they would reflect, they must think it an unreasonable liberty to take with the child of a friend: the world is sharp-sighted enough in discovering every person's faults; but for a parent to proclaim them, is absurd and cruel. In the other case, let them examine the state of their own knowledge, and how they came by it, and they will abate in their expectations; besides it should never be forgotten, that success in life is not the certain lot of understanding, nor is great learning the source of happiness; and that the highest degree of school acquirements, is often vain and frivolous.

Young persons, who make the best figure at school, are too apt to imagine they have done all that is necessary, and grow idle; whereas, those who are slower in their acquirements, if they incline to pursue their studies at a riper age, soon leave them behind. The learning attained before twenty years of age, is productive of little useful knowledge, if it is not cultivated afterwards by study and reflection.

The minds of children are flexible and ready to receive any impressions; but is it therefore, necessary to fix in them the names

of

of kings, rivers and cities, that have no longer any exiftence? I have feen a boy at feven years of age able to read in Homer; in which I found nothing to admire but the abfurdity of his father, who had himfelf taken the pains to torture the child's mind and memory to fo vain a purpofe : fuch little prodigies raife the felf-conceit of their preceptors, who in return plant arrogance in the minds of their pupils. There is better encouragement to a father's hopes in a child that is ignorant, than in one that is vain ; for vanity is a quality that is very apt to increafe, whereas ignorance diminifhes daily.

There is no fear of children's minds fuffering for want of employment, they will conftantly be at work, and profitably to, if they are allowed the ufe of their natural endowments; free from fetters, and that conftant oppofition they meet with in moft kinds of Education.

Children have a will of their own on all occafions, equally with thofe who think that they have a better right to it; and which, like their elders, they maintain more or lefs ftrenuoufly, according to their difpofitions. Lord Chefterfield's fon, would poffibly

sibly have preferred the hangman's office, to that of acting in a public character abroad; which was pressed upon him by his father, who had not thought proper to consult his disposition, or paid no respect to to it, in this matter. He mistakes the business of Education, who thinks that his opinions are always to be received on account of his wisdom, or authority; for either of these urged improperly, will but increase the opposition. This is no fault in the child, it is human nature; his father had it before him. Many rising inclinations subside if unnoticed or managed with address, that would grow incorrigible by opposition.

Indolence and carelesness seem to be vices natural to children; but they disappear in their sports and play, where they are seen to be lively, full of application, exact observers of rule and symmetry, and will set up and pull down many times, and not pardon the least fault in each other, that tends to defeat the completion of their design. When learning is therefore made their choice and amusement, it is no wonder that they should draw more profit from it, than can be extracted by the fear of chastisement, which
makes

makes them hate their book as the chief cause of all their unhappiness.

> *Hoc patrium est, potius consuefacere filium*
> *Sua sponte recte facere, quam alieno metu.*
> *Hoc pater ac dominus interest: hoc qui nequit,*
> *Fateatur nescire imperare liberis.*
>
> Ter. Adelp.

The restraints and attentions required in Education are sufficiently irksome to children; the gentlest means should therefore be employed, to engage assiduity; and if correction be necessary, it should be administered with the reluctant tenderness of a parent, and the kind expostulations of a friend, and not inflicted with the countenance of a fiend, and the lash of a hard-hearted taskmaster. If they have a due sense of their fault, there is no need of correction; and if they defy correction, little good is to be expected; and the more frequent the use of it, the more obstinate and hardened they be-

---

* Tis a father's part to use his child so, that his own choice, rather than outward constraint, may put him upon doing well. Here lies the difference between a father and a master, and he that does otherwise, let him own, that he knows nothing of what belongs to the government of children.

come. There are but small hopes to be entertained of those children, who cannot bear indulgence; I mean by indulgence, an opposite behaviour to that eternal teasing and severity, so often practised.

Education is useless where there is no confidence; children know better than any body when they deserve chastisement, and seldom deserve more than they fear; they know exactly if they are punished with propriety, and receive great damage from chastisement wrongfully inflicted. I have taken the trouble to examine into the causes of some disturbances in the very great schools, called rebellions; and I have always found them to originate in the master's improper behaviour.

The benefits of Education flow from the right proceedings of the instructor; from his knowledge of human nature; and his inculcating that knowledge which is the result of his experience in the affairs of the world. In this view it may be said, that "Education forms the Man."

You remember the young *****, the eldest at eleven, the youngest at nine years of age.

age. Thefe boys had never been at fchool, and had been brought up with an unremitted tendernefs and moft unlimited indulgence. They had been taught to read by their mother; and, from a perfon who attended them three times in a week, for an hour only each time they could, in about three years, render any French book into Englifh at fight, in correct, good language. At this period they entered upon the ufe of the grammar rules, for the conftruction of the French tongue. They were taught Latin in the fame way, beginning with Latin and Englifh books after a flight knowledge of the declenfions of nouns and conjugations of verbs, and in lefs than two years, they had read through the Georgics and every book of the Æneid; fome Ovid and other books. The three firft years at fchools are thrown away on grammar; but by acquiring a trifling knowledge of the language, by fentences of eafy conftruction, the application of the grammar rules become intelligible; whereas when adminiftered in the ufual method, they are beyond the reach of children, and tend rather to ftupify than illuminate their conceptions. If any one doubts of this, let him read over his Lilly's grammar; there can be no reafon why, in great fchools, they

are

are refused the use of Latin and English books to assist them in construction, but that they would acquire the language faster than the masters wish they should.*

Grammar

---

* At Dessau, in Germany, there is an institution for the education of youth, and for making the foundation of learning easy and agreeable, with little constraint, and in a manner which joins the *dulce* to the real *utile*.

Many questions having arisen concerning the practicability of this scheme, and the real progress of instruction obtained by this new method, several persons of learning attended, from different parts of Germany, (May 13, 14, 15.—1776.) at Dessau, to examine into the progress of the scholars; an account of which examination, is given in the Berlin Review, vol. 29, part II.

Boys of seven and eight years of age, who had been in that institution a year or a year and a half, were heard, not only to prattle French and Latin very currently, but it was found that they actually understood good Latin.

Divers of the examiners opened classic authors, wherever they pleased, and the boys translated them directly; reading their translation out of the Latin book as if it had been translated for them on a written paper.

Several of the learned strangers present, examined them, in Latin, with regard to any passages in ancient or modern history; to which, the boys gave satisfactory
answers,

Grammar may be compared to finging, in which many arrive at a refpectable execution without the knowledge of notes or compofition. How many perfons write and exprefs themfelves elegantly in their vernacular tongue, by practical obfervations only ! we fpeak of grammar as if every body underftood it, but I am fafe in afferting, that there are, as few grammarians, in the ftrict fenfe of the word, as there are good poets : but good fenfe and attention can never fail of attaining a knowledge of any language, fufficient for every purpofe.

The Greek philofophers, of all the different fects

anfwers, on the fpot, in Latin. It was the fame in arithmetic, geometry, and trigonometry, which were folved by the boys with that readinefs, that might have been expected from profeffed mafters.

The ftrangers are amazed at their progrefs, on account of the fhortnefs of the time, and the little reftraint put upon the children ; as it has been all effected amidft cheerfulnefs, and continual variety of bodily exercife.

The names of the mafters are, Bafedon, Wolke, Simon, and Schweighaufer. I honour thefe men, tho' I do not know them. I honour too the prince of Deffau, for the encouragement which he has given to the inftitution.

MONTHLY REVIEW, *Sept.* 1777.

sects or schools, were unanimous in decrying the methods used by the grammarians, in teaching the youth at Athens; they began with putting Homer into their hands, because, as they said poetry was written before prose: and there is no doubt but their fellow-labourers of this day, would reason as well in defence of their modes, and would not deign to give any answer, if they were asked, how a knowledge of the mother tongue was acquired?

The boys, I mentioned, had pencils given to them at a very early age for their amusement; the consequence was, that when you saw them, they could delineate any thing they saw or read a description of, had a tolerable notion of light and shade, and laying on water colours; and all this as a matter of pastime, without the assistance of any drawing-master. Writing, which is a kind of drawing, was the work of a month only. With each a map of the world, they had made themselves so good geographers, that there are but few men who have so complete a knowledge of the surface of the globe.

Their father's plan was never to hurry, or urge any thing seriously; and he declared that

that he oftner interferred to draw them off, by fome trifling amufement, than to engage their attention to whatever he wifhed them to acquire. Your obfervation, that they would be men without ever having been children, is juft; their fpirits having never been depreffed by the violence of a foolifhly conducted fubordination. The grand *defideratum*, is, to give children a difpofition to ftudy and reflection, that they may profit by it when they go into the world, and are of an age to learn.

It is no very uncommon thing to fee children who, at the earlieft age, difcover a difpofition to be managed without feverity, and whom the moft extenfive indulgence can never induce to any vicious inclinations : for good difpofitions will make every return to franknefs and confidence. How cruel is it to break fuch generous noble fpirits by a favage and tyrannical behaviour !

Thofe parents who have good reafon to fufpect the frowardnefs of their ftock, are excufable in turning them over to the tormentors; as are thofe alfo, who are confcious that they may exhibit fome things to their obfervation, which may not exactly correfpond with what is absolutely necessary to a good Education.

They who insist on the usefulness of great schools, say, that the meek will there acquire spirit and sharpness, to fit them for the world, as they call it; whereas it is notorious, that encouragement is the lot, only, of the bold and forward. It is in the company of men of good breeding, after leaving school, that the gentle shake off their timidity; and for the sharpness of a school boy, it is generally founded in ill-mannerly rapaciousness. Another of their arguments is, that sheepishness or bashfulness must always accompany a private Education; and so it may if the children are under improper management. But it is certain, that where such a tendency arises, as it generally does, from a constitutional debility of nerves, they stand a better chance to shake it off, by an attention directed to it under the parent's eye, than from the total neglect of it at schools. Weak nerves can never be cured by bustle and violence; but by a proper treatment may be much assisted. As to bashfulness, where it is not from a constitutional defect, let me give you a familiar instance

ſtance, that it has nothing to do with ſchool Education: the quakers do not ſend their children from home, and yet I am confident that you never ſaw a baſhful young quaker; and rarely a forward, impudent one. And here I will do the quakers the juſtice to obſerve, that I think them the moſt reaſonably living, and the happieſt people in the kingdom.

Is it not ſtrange, that old as our planet is, it ſhould be the conſtant rule of Education, to conduct children to the end propoſed, by unworthy means? either jealouſy, fear, envy, or vanity, all of which grow into vices of the moſt unhappy tendencies, is planted in the heart, to cheriſh whatever is offered as inſtruction for the head.

I am certain that the uſual method which confines youth to intenſe and tedious application, to attempt to gain a grammatical knowledge of the dead languages, which they never uſe, is abſurd, as well as the puzzling them with hiſtories of times wholly inapplicable to their own. The ſame time beſtowed on their vernacular tongue; the French language; on the knowledge of ſomething that might be uſeful or amuſing, excited by their curioſity or natural inclination;

or on things relative to their future bufinefs in life, would be fure to produce a lafting benefit: all thefe things are natural in a home Education. Good manners, and other amiable qualities attained under the conftant attention and example of their parents, and their acquaintance, will lay the foundation of all proper acquirements, better than can be done by any prefent fyftem of fchool Education; which generally confifts in an affectation of doing great things, by means totally inadequate and impertinent.

To a young man, brought up as I have propofed, a few months application, after fifteen with a preceptor, if he is intended for one of the learned profeffions, will make him mafter of Latin and Greek, enough to inform himfelf of all that is neceffary to fit him for either of the univerfities; and being untainted with vice or habits of idlenefs, he cannot fail of profiting, in the fulleft manner, in whatever may be the object of his wifhes and endeavours.

Many parents, who had promifed themfelves happinefs from friendfhips with their children, which perhaps fociety had failed to furnifh, have fuffered difappointments, and

and charged their blameless children with ingratitude. If the foundation of that felicity is laid at an early time, by the proper care and attention of the parents, there is no reason to fear that the remembrance of it will be effaced. The mother, whose breasts have been the delight and support of her children, shall have them cheered in the evening of her days, with reverence and love; as shall the father who has manifested his right to it, by an affectionate discharge of his duty, in superintending their Education.*

On the subject before us, the world is too apt to reason, as in most other cases, from general maxims, which lead us perpetually into errors; but here it is particularly to be noted, that there cannot be two cases alike, so that hints only are to be expected. This indeed may be insisted upon, that where

* Some parents expect that the anxiety and care they feel on account of their children, should, in them, produce a like tenderness, and should be always in their memory. This cannot be, from the nature of youth. They ought rather to think, that in a faithful discharge of their own duty, they repay what they were indebted to their parents, on a like account: and thus parental kindness is handed down from generation to generation.

a father

a father will do all he can, it muſt have better ſucceſs, than from any other perſon; becauſe the intereſt the father has in his ſon, and the reciprocal attachment, can never take place in another man.

I think you will allow me to have kept my word in not propoſing any thing with a view to a general plan of Education: but if only fifty young men in a year, throughout the kingdom, are ſent into ſociety on the plan I have ventured to propoſe, I have no doubt, but they will be happier themſelves, and as far as example goes, will be more uſeful to others, than can be expected from the common methods of enſlaving and debaſing the mind.

Writers on general Education fall into one and the ſame error; they want to change the order of nature, whoſe delight is variety; they forget that in the numbers of families which form an empire, there are no two ſituations exactly alike; and of courſe what may be proper, or to the mind of one, will be rejected by another. The late biſhop of Autun has written a treatiſe on public inſtruction, publiſhed by the order of the national aſſembly in France; wherein he ſays as much as is
neceſſary

neceffary to enforce a public education : nevertheless, what he propofes would have an ill effect were it practicable.

The happinefs of a people depends more on its manners, than on any other thing; which above all, are improved and preferved in purity, by induftry. What would a wider diffufion, of what is called learning, do in this country? to anfwer this by afking another queftion, have we not more writers and readers than are neceffary? it is this polifh that is one of the caufes, that fo few in the kingdom are now to be found in their right place, or under that defcription to which they naturally belong.

Such learning as would probably follow a general and uniform Education, would fill a nation, with conceited, idle babblers, and with confufion. If fuch a fpirit of induftry could be fo generally planted in every bofom, among the common people, that a man, when he had finifhed his day's labour, would be ready to go half a mile to help a friend, he would be much better employed, than in talking of what can never concern him. In America, where they are great readers, I have feen four men on the roof
of

of a houſe employed on a newſpaper, and not completing that in a day, which two Engliſh labourers would have done.

Some men have the good fortune to in-creaſe their content from knowledge; but is by no means a general ſource of happi-neſs: but for the herd who are to plow, ſow, fight battles by ſea and land, and live by the ſweat of their brow, which eminent-ly ſuits the natural poſition of our iſland, the great maxim to be inculcated is, *La-bor omnia vincit.*

I am Dear Sir, &c. &c.

CONCISE ACCOUNT

OF THE

RISE AND PROGRESS

OF THE

ENGLISH CONSTITUTION,

FROM THE CONQUEST.

CONCISE ACCOUNT

OF THE

RISE AND PROGRESS

OF THE

ENGLISH CONSTITUTION,

FROM THE CONQUEST.

THE Feudal law is the basis of the political government and of the jurisprudence, established by the Normans in this country; the nature of which, in the outlines, every person is acquainted with.

Attachment naturally follows the possession of a portion of land, accompanied with the idea of property; both of which tend to make the possessor forgetful of the dependance and conditions annexed to the original grant. It seems equitable, that he who sows should reap; hence fiefs, at first precarious, were made annual. Building, planting, and other improvements, extended the expectation of further favour; hence they were next granted for a term of years. To expel a man who had fulfilled all his engagements, and the conditions on which he originally received the fief, seemed hard; hence, in a subsequent period, the chieftains demanded the enjoyment of the feudal lands during life. It was discovered, that in battle a man would more readily hazard his life, if his family was sure of inheriting his possessions; hence fiefs became hereditary, and descended, during one age, to the son; then to the grandson, next to the brothers, and afterwards to more distant relations. The idea of property stole in gradually upon that of military pay, which was the first intention, and each century made some addition to the stability of fiefs and tenures.

In this history of acquisitions, the power of the prince suffered: the chieftain sure to be backed by his rascals, who were to be sharers, boldly advanced new pretensions; till at length, too powerful to apprehend any thing from the sovereign, they secured by law, what they had acquired by usurpasion; till in the end, those titles were preferred to allodial

allodial or free titles: the firſt was an aſſociation of force and protection; the other ſtood alone, and were at laſt driven to the neceſſity of reſigning their poſſeſſions into the hands of the king, or ſome perſon of power and valour, and received them back with the condition of feudal ſervices. Thus the political government was devoured by the feudal, and the kingdom divided into baronies, and thoſe into inferior fiefs.

The king was ſupreme lord of the landed property; and all poſſeſſions were conceived to be, in ſome degree, a ſpecies of benefice. As the vaſſal owed ſtated ſervices to the baron, ſo the baron himſelf did to the crown; the vaſſal was bound to defend his baron in war, the baron at the head of his vaſſals, to fight in defence of the king and the kingdom. Beſides the military ſervices, there were others impoſed of a civil nature.

If the king wanted more from the barons than were due from their tenures, he was obliged to aſſemble them and aſk their advice and conſent; for at that time, men bred to arms, would not be governed by the abſolute will of another. In one view, the barons

rons confidered this attendance as a privilege; in another, as a burden: the expence, and leaving their domeftic affairs, made them wifh to be exempted. On the other hand, the king wifhed to have a full affembly; the chief badge of their fubordination to the crown: befides, a thin meeting had lefs authority with the public at large, in its determinations.

It was the fame with the barons in their courts: the kingdom was a great barony; a barony, the epitome of a fmall kingdom: but the vaffals fell under a greater fubordination to their lords, than the baron himfelf under his fovereign, and that from a natural tendency, from his riches, hofpitality, and a variety of things productive of authority. If the king acquired any addition to his power in war, he was fure to lofe it in the intervals of peace and tranquility: the baron could demand redrefs; the vaffal had no appeal from the court of barony. Such was the ftate of the government under the firft Norman princes.

When the ancient fabric of the Saxon legiflature was fubverted, and the natives fubdued by William, his authority over the barons confolidated

confolidated the whole into one compact body; the barons were eafily managed while they remained as an army, from whence fome have paffed great eulogiums on his fortune and abilities : it was afterward a different tafk ; when the barons were fettled in their caftles and coalefced with the people, the king was then only the greateft baron, and then perfonal vigour and ability were requifite in the fovereign.

The power of the kings of England, however increafed, whilft that of fome other princes, which had the fame origin, was leffened; and though it appears but little analogous at firft view, the power of the crown, was the firft caufe of the prefent conftitution. The kingdom of France, with a like feudal origin, funk gradually under the moft abfolute monarchy, whilft this kingdom attained the fummit of liberty. In France the royal authority was inconfiderable; the lord's, every thing; the bulk of the people accounted for nothing; being the flaves of their lords, they were engaged in their quarrels amongft each other, and againft their fovereign, without any chance of receiving advantage. When the time arrived

that

that the lords were fwallowed, one by one, by the predominant power of the reigning prince, the few privileges that had been granted to the lower orders, were little refpected by a fovereign who had entered into no engagement on that account, and found himfelf in a condition to impofe his will, and preferve his authority.

In England the exceffive power of the king was the caufe of general freedom; it there excited a fpirit of union and co-refiftance. The different orders of the feudal government were connected on other terms than in France; by which means the fpirit of liberty pervaded the whole mafs. We apprehend that it may thus be accounted for, that in France, the lords were the old and accuftomed territorical mafters of the people; whereas, the Normans being ftrangers, they oppofed the fovereign, were obliged to court their under-tenants, and let them participate in the advantages which accrued. By degrees the people infifted, that every individual fhould be entitled to the protection of the law; and thus did thofe rights, in which the lords had intrenched themfelves, become
a bulwark

a bulwark of defence to the people, both againſt the king and the barons.

In forty years after the conqueſt, and in the reign of the firſt Henry, the cauſes mentioned began to ſhow their effect; for this Prince having aſcended the throne, to the excluſion of his elder brother, was obliged to reſort to the affection of his ſubjects: he mitigated the rigour of the feudal laws, but on condition, that the ſame ſhould extend to their reſpective vaſſals. The Curfeu and other heavy laws on the people, eſtabliſhed by the Conquerer, were aboliſhed.

Under Henry the ſecond, the ancient trial by jury made its appearance again, though imperfectly. But it was under the deſpotiſm of John, that the full force of this effect was ſeen, by a general confederacy being formed againſt him, which obliged him to ſubmit himſelf to the diſpoſal of his ſubjects, who exacted from him that famous charter, called Magna Charta. The great charter, was, as it were, a general banner ſet up for the perpetual union of all claſſes of the people, and the foundation on which all equitable laws were to be conſtructed.

Under

Under the reign of Henry the third, the various conflicts between him and his barons, were all terminated with an increase of importance to the people, who obtained new privileges by the statutes of Merton and Marlebridge.

Under Edward the first, in thirteen years only, the laws arrived at once at perfection, from the wisdom of the prince, who saw that a strict administration of justice would curb the turbulent nobility, and conciliate the people. This era affords the first instance of a *legal* admission of the deputies of towns and boroughs into parliament, for the purpose of raising subsidies.*

Edward

* The same thing had been usurped by Leicester in the former reign.

From the conquest to this period it was the destiny of the people of France, to be the slaves of their numerous and haughty nobility; for though they had assemblies of the general estates, something resembling our parliaments, which admitted deputies from some towns, under the title of the third estate, yet as they were from particular parts of the king's domain, no influence accrued to the people; so far from it, that it soon became a maxim there, *que vent le roi, si vent la loi;* the will of the king, is the will of the law.

The people opposed the oppression and insults of
their

Edward was obliged to confirm the great charter no lefs than eleven times during his reign; but he converted a precarious privilege into an eftablifhed law; for in the ftatute, *de tallagio non concedendo*, it is decreed, that no tax fhall be laid, or impoft levied, without the joint confent of the lords and commons. This was the engine with which the people were thenceforth enabled to oppofe

their haughty nobility in 1357, at Beauvais; but it terminated in the deftruction of fome thoufands of them: in their fimplicity they faw no remedy but in the eftablifhment of the regal power, which might reduce their oppreffors to the fame level with themfelves; and the nobility having never cultivated their affection, had nothing to oppofe to the gradual advances of the royal authority; fo that in the reign of Louis the eleventh, the general eftates were abolifhed.

The French parliaments do not comprehend the meeting of the eftates of the kingdom, but are courts of juftice. The edicts of the king, refpecting any part of his government of the realm, are there regiftered, to give them the force of a law. If the act is thought grievous to the fubject, the parliament can reject it; on a prefumption that they are not fatisfied that it is the king's will. If he infifts, he comes there in perfon, and holds what is called a bed of juftice; declares the ordinance to be his, and it is accordingly regiftered. Each province has its parliament, and all of them are under the fuperintendance of that of Paris.

pose, and make legal conquests over the authority of the crown.

Under the second Edward, the commons began to annex petitions to the subsidy bills; and under Edward the third, they declared they would not acknowledge any law to which they had not expresly assented. They impeached and procured the condemnation of some of the first ministers of state. In the reign of Henry the fourth, the commons refused to grant subsidies till their petitions had been answered. Under Henry the fifth, the nation was engaged in wars against France; and in the turbulent reign of Henry the sixth, the laws were silenced amidst the quarrels of the houses of York and Lancaster.

Henry the seventh mounted the throne with something of the appearance of a conqueror. He had promises to fulfil, and injuries to avenge; the people had been worried out, and abhorred all idea of resistance; and the almost exterminated nobility, was left defenceless to the mercy of the sovereign. The commons, who had acted only a second part, were afraid to form an opposition, without the assistance of their accustomed leaders; they therefore purchased such security as they could get under the Tudors, at the expence

pence of liberty; and England seemed to submit in its turn to the fate of all the other nations in Europe. But the advantages they had tasted, had made too sensible an impression to be forgotten, and they soon vindicated the right of granting, or rather as they used it, of refusing subsidies: they clung obstinately to this plank of the wreck, which was destined to prove the instrument of their preservation.

Under Edward the sixth, the tyrannical laws against treason, framed by Henry the eight, were abolished; but Mary was enabled by her fanaticism, and that of a part of her subjects, to astonish the world with her cruelties to the rest.

In the long and brilliant reign of Elizabeth, England began to breathe anew; and, the protestant religion being again seated on the throne, brought with it some freedom and toleration. The tyranny of the star chamber however continued, and the inquisitional tribunal of the high commission court was even established; but pity for the former sufferings of the queen, her great talents, and the glory of her reign, served to justify and excuse her to her subjects, and in spite of her principles of government, have ranked her among the greatest sovereigns,

The nation recovered from its lethargy under the Stuarts. James the first was imprudent enough to make an ostentatious display of what his predecessors had been content to enjoy, by keeping it confined to the cabinet; which alarmed the people, and revived an opposition to the sovereign, which had been long dormant. The storms which had been some time gathering, burst with all its vengeance upon Charles the first. The notions that had heretofore formed a spirit to attack the established faith, directed itself to politics, with the same inflexible obstinacy: the commons were complete in the knowlege of the state of the nation, and of their own force; and Charles had to cope with a nation put in motion, and directed by an assembly of crafty statesmen. The compulsory loans and taxes, called benevolences, were declared contrary to law. Arbitrary imprisonments and martial law were abolished, and the court of high-commission and the star-chamber suppressed, and in the conflict, at length, the king perished. The people

ple were amazed awhile, with the chimera of the authority of all, which foon manifefted itfelf in the tyranny of a few; and they, at laft, reforted to the general principles of their former conftitution, and invited over Charles the fecond.

On this occafion the fame jealoufy was called forth to watch the like intemperance of prerogative in him, that had caufed all the troubles of the former reign. The eagernefs of Charles betrayed his projects, and the people refolved to remove all remnants of defpotifm : the remains of ancient feudal tenures were abolifhed, the law againft heretics repealed, and the Habeas Corpus act eftablifhed.

James the fecond followed openly the fame project that had proved fatal to his family ; and that on a more enlarged fcale, although the execution of any thing which tended to exalt the royal prerogative, had been daily becoming more and more impracticable. But the people of England were now fo well grounded in the conduct of their interefts, that the depriving James of his crown was accomplifhed without any terrible convulfion, and even by a fhort and eafy operation:
it

it appears a singular event in the annals of mankind, both with respect to its moderation and legality. The breaches that had been made in the constitution were repaired, and new buttresses constructed, by taking this opportunity to form an original and express compact between king and people. A more precise oath was exacted from the new king. It was determined, that to impose taxes without the consent of parliament, or to keep a standing army in time of peace, are contrary to law; the power exerted formerly by the crown of dispensing with the laws, was abolished; and a right in the subject to present petitions to the king, was established; and a declaration of some other articles, formed, what was called the bill of rights, and became an act of parliament in the first year of William and Mary; and the liberty of the press was established four years after.

The great charter marked out the limits in which the royal authority ought to be confined, and must be considered as the first grand era in the history of the Constitution; the second was in the reign of Edward the first, when a few outworks were raised; but it is in the third grand era, at the revolution, that the fortification was completed.

A SUCCINCT

CHRONOLOGICAL

HISTORY OF FRANCE.

TRANSLATED AND *ABRIDGED*

FROM THE

FRENCH OF MONS. HENAULT.

A SUCCINCT

CHRONOLOGICAL

HISTORY of FRANCE.

TRANSLATED and *ABRIDGED*

FROM THE

FRENCH of MONS. HENAULT.

FIRST RACE.

509.

PARIS made the Capital of France.

511.

Clovis, the firſt King, died, after reigning — Years.

562.

Clotharius, the ſecond Prince who reigned alone, died at Compeigne.

613.

Clotharius II. was the third Prince who reigned alone. 617. Holds a kind of moveable

able parliaments, called *Placita*; from whence the word Pleas is derived. 628. Dies greatly regretted.

Commencement of the Mahometan Æra, called Hegira, or the Date of the Flight of Mahomet, from Mecca, 622. He died of poison in 632.

628.

Dagobert, the third sole King of France. Incredible Riches brought into France by the Levant Trade. 638. Died at Epinay. The Royal Authority absorbed by the Power of the Mayors of the Palace.

688.

Thierry III. reigns alone. Pepin defeats him and usurps the whole Authority, under the Title of Mayor of the Palace.

692.

Clovis III. Son of Thierry; under whose name Pepin continued to reign.

695.

Childerbert III. his Brother; in whose name also Pepin continued to reign. Dies in 711.

Dagobert

711.

Dagobert III. Pepin died in 714. The Saracens difpoffefs the Vifigoths of Spain, who had got footing in 400.

716.

Chilperic II. but fubject to the Authority of Charles Martel, the Mayor.

720.

Thierry IV. furnamed of Chilles. Died in 737. Charles Martel continued to Reign as Duke of the French; and dies in 741.

741.

Carloman and Pepin fhare the Government. Pepin puts an end to the Interregnum, by filling the Throne with

742.

Childeric III. Council of Leftines, which was the firft in which they began to reckon the years from the Incarnation of our Lord. Dionyfius Exiguus was the Author. 743. Childeric was dethroned, fhaved, and put up in the abby of Sithin, now St. Bertin, and died in 754. The end of the Race of Merovingians; after a fpace of 270 Years, computing from Clovis.

Mayor of the Palace, was called *Major Domus Regiæ, Palatii Gubernator, Præfectus,* &c. And afterwards, when at the head of Armies, *Dux Francorum, Dux et Princeps, sub-regulus.* Kings and Princes of the blood at this time wore their Hair long, (a German Custom) so that to render one incapable of Reigning, they shaved him. The general language was Latin.

Second Race.

751.

Pepin proclaimed at Soissons.

768.

Charlemain and Carloman succeeds their Father. 771. Carloman dies. 774. Extinction of the Kingdom of the Lombards (which had lasted 206 years) in the person of Disiderius, who was beat by Charlemain, who succeeded him as King. 788. The Dutchy of Bavaria united to the Crown of France. 799. Charlemain seized the Islands of Majorca and Minorca. 800. Crowned Emperor of the West by Pope Leo III. The King of Persia resigns the Holy Land to the Emperor.

The

The Cuftom of the Judgment of the Crofs, confifted in a determination in favour of him who could hold his arms extended in form of a Crofs longer than his Antagonift.

813. Makes his fon Louis Colleague with him in the Empire. 817. Creates his fon Lotharius, his Colleague, Pepin, King of Aquitaine; and Louis, King of Bavaria. 819. Title of Vifcount came to be known in the Perfon of Cixiline, Vifcount of Narbonne. Vidame. Vice-dominus. 830. Charles the Bald, Son by his fecond wife Judith, together with the other brothers, ftrip him of his Dominions; he is obliged to take fhelter in a Convent, but afterwards reftored. 833. His three Sons confpire again; feize his Perfon, and oblige him to abdicate. 834. He is again Reftored by divifions among the Sons. 837. Finding himfelf Declining, he made a new partition, without naming a Succeffor. He was the talleft and ftrongeft Man of his time. The famous Rowland was one of his Officers.

840.
Charles II. furnamed the Bald. 877. Died at Brios, poifoned by a jew phyfician,
Zedechias;

Zedechias; in whom he placed the greatest confidence. He gave a deadly blow to the royal authority by making dignities and titles hereditary. He had the title of most Christian King conferred on him by the Council of Savonnieres in 859. Pepin and Charles stiled themselves Kings by Divine Clemency; whereas the Kings of the third Race stile themselves Kings by the Grace of God; as well with regard to Religion as to signify their independency on the Pope.

877.

Louis II. surnamed the Stammerer; Son of Charles the Bald by his first wife. He was obliged by Factions to dismember his Demesnes, which gave rise to the Dukes of Britanny and Burgundy, and the Counts of Anjou and Provence.

879.

Louis III. and Carloman. 882. Louis dies. Carloman is killed by a Wild Boar.

884.

Charles the Fat, at that time Emperor. Dies without issue the contempt of his people.

Eudes,

888.

Eudes, Count of Paris, takes possession in preference to Charles the Simple; who, however, kept the Country between the Seine and the Meux. Dies at la Ferre, aged 40.

898.

Charles the Simple. The Imperial Dignity is transferred from the House of France, by his weakness, and becomes Elective. The great Offices, which before had been only Commissions, were rendered hereditary, because the Empire had ceased to be so; and a Prince elected must submit to conditions imposed by the Electors. Neustria, now called Normandy, granted to the Normans. 922. He is Defeated by Eudes, who was himself killed; and Charles is confined in the Castle of Peronne, and dies in 929.

Rodolph Duke of Burgundy, brother-in-law to Hugh the Great, who refused the Crown, succeeds Charles after his defeat by Eudes. He is obliged to distribute great part of the Crown Lands among the Grandees. This is the Era of the first Institution of Feifs, although some feint Traces may be perceived before this time.

936.

Louis IV. furnamed Tranfmarine from his Mother's having carried him to England, upon his Father, Charles the Simple, being made a Prifoner. Died at Rheims.

954.

Lothaire. He had been affociated with his father three years before his Death. Succeeded to the Crown at the Age of fifteen, under the Protection of Hugh the Great. Died of Poifon at Rheims.

986.

Louis V. furnamed the Slothful, reigned but one year, and died of Poifon at Compeigne. His Uncle fhould have fucceeded by right, but Hugh Capet feized the Crown. The end of the Carlovingian Race, which lafted 236 Years.

In the laft Century, the Tongue was changed from Latin to what is called the Romance Tongue; that is, a mixture of the Frank dialect and bad Latin. There was alfo the Teudefque, or Teutonic, introduced by the Franks: this appears by a Treaty between Charles the Bald and Louis the Germanic. Here the two Languages are very diftinct;

the

the Tudefque is for the Germans, and the Romance for the Franks: this is the moft ancient Record in France. Towards the end of the fecond Race, the Kingdom was held by the Law of Feudal Tenures, and Governed rather as a great Fief than a Monarchy.

Third Race.

987.

Hugh Capet, the Founder of the Third Race, fucceeded in perference to Charles Duke of Lorrain, fon to Louis Transmarine, and uncle to Louis V. 991. Caufes his fon Robert to be Crowned with him. This is the age of Ignorance.

996.

Robert, Crowned at Orleans, aged 25. Concubines, that were allowed to the Clergy, were not what we mean by that word, for then they would have been contrary to Divine Law; but founded on a Roman Cuftom, of having a Concubine at the fame time with a Wife: it was *Semi-matrimonium*, and the Concubine *Semi-conjux*, and was a legitimate union, though perhaps not underftood underſtood at this time in its full extent. In 1022 a Pope was elected of only eighteen Years of Age. Robert refuſes the Empire and Kingdom of Italy, both offered to him.

1031.

Henry I. He had been Crowned in his Father's life-time. The Emperors began to have their Sons created King of the Romans, in imitation, poſſibly, of Charlemain, who had been firſt created King of the Romans; but they kept this Cuſtom, after they were deprived of the Kingdom of Italy, by way of creating a kind of hereditary Right to the Empire, by pointing out to the people who were to fill the Throne when vacant.

1060.

Philip I. eight Years of Age. 1105. He aſſociates his ſon Louis, ſurnamed Craſſus or the Groſs, with him in the Regal Dignity.

1108.

Louis VI. or Le Gros, in a Quarrel with the Emperor, Henry V. the Clergy joined the reſt of his Vaſſals, and Suger, Abbot of St.

St. Dennis brought his Subjects to his Sovereign, together with a Banner of a Crimson Colour fix'd to a Gilt Lance, and called Oriflamme. This Prince began to recover the Authority usurped by the Vassals, by establishing the Commons, or third Estate.

1137.

Louis VII. surnamed the Young. About this year the Code of Justinian was found in Apulia, and became the written Law of France. Abelard died in 1142, and Eloisa in 1163. The Guelphs and Gibellines, two factious Parties in Italy, took their Rise in this Reign: the former were attached to the Pope, the latter to the Emperor. In this Century are perceived the first Traces of Theatrical Representations, in a Species of Devotional Tragedy, being the Miracles of St. Catherine: it was set on foot by Geoffry, afterwards Abbot of St. Alban's, in England. The representation of Mysteries, generally looked upon as the first of this kind, did not take place till 1398. And in this Century were established Schools in Cathedral Churches, and Monasteries; to whom we are indebted for the preservation of almost

moſt all the Works of the Ancients: the Monks employing themſelves in tranſcribing Books. In this Century, France, and other Chriſtian States began to uſe Coats of Arms.

1180.

Philip II. aged fifteen, ſurnamed Auguſtus. This is one of the moſt Victorious Princes. He checked the power of the Nobles and expelled the Jews, releaſing his ſubjects from all Debts due to them. A ſtrange Revolution happened to Henry the Emperor, ſurnamed the Lion: His Territories extended from the Adriatic Gulph to the Baltic; he was ſtripped of all by the Emperor Frederic, nothing more remaining to his family than the Dutchy of Brunſwic, which they now poſſeſs. From this Duke Henry, by Matilda, is deſcended King George the third of England. In 1214 it was that a Marſhal of France firſt commanded an Army. Henry Clement at the Battle of Bovines, againſt the Emperor Otho and his Allies, to the amount of 150,000 Men. The origin of Serjeants at Arms. The firſt Guards of the Kings of France diſtinguiſhed themſelves at this Battle. Philip ſubdued, and united to the Brown, Normandy, Anjou,

jou, Maine, Touraine, Poitou, Auvergne, Vermandois, Artois, &c.

1223.

Louis VIII. furnamed Cœur de Lion. He reigned three Years.

1226.

Louis IX. called St. Louis, aged 12 Years. This was the third Minority in the third Race. The time of his Minority was confumed in Subduing the confederate Princes and Barons. 1241. Was formed the Affociation of the Hans Towns, for the protection of their Commerce. In 1245, in the Affembly of Lions, the Red Hat was appropriated to Cardinals. 1254. An Ordinance of St. Louis dated from St. Gilles. The three Eftates were confulted in matters relative to the Interefts of the People. On one fide of the King's Coin was a Crofs, and on the Reverfe, Pillars; from whence to this day, the different fides of a piece of Money are called Crofs and Pile. Eftablifhment of the Police at Paris by Stephen Boileau. Inftitution of the Military Order of the Ship and Crefcent.

1270.

Philip III. called the Hardy. The firft

letters of Ennoblement granted to Raoul the Goldsmith. The laws of Appanage began to be better understood: instead of dismembering the Demesnes, Grants were made for a particular time, which again reverted to the crown; 'till Philip the Fair, they continued in the Females; but by his codicil, the county of Anjou, granted to his youngest Son, reverted to the Crown for want of Male Heirs.

1285.

Philip IV. called the Fair, aged seventeen Years. The first letters for creating a Dutchy and Peerage, were granted to John duke of Brittany, 1297. 1308. The prohibition of Duels in Civil Causes. It was the Institution of Parliaments, says Loyseau, that prevented our being Cantoned and Dismembered after the manner of Italy and Germany, and that maintained the Kingdom intire.

1314.

Louis X. called Hutin, Mutinous and Quarrelsome, twenty-four Years of Age.

1316.

Philip V. the Long, twenty three years of Age.

1322.

Charles IV. the Fair; twenty-six Years old. Bourbon erected into a Dukedom.

1328.

Philip VI. of Valois. Inftitution of the Gabelle or Salt Tax in this Reign. Pope John XXII. died in 1344, aged ninety. He added the third Crown to the Pontifical Tiara. Pope Hormifdas ufed the firft, and Boniface VIII. added a fecond.

1350.

John, aged thirty Years. His fon Charles is the firft who bore the title of Dauphin, and was made Duke of Normandy. So great were the variations of Coin in this reign, that from one day to another they fcarce knew what Payment they were to make.

1364.

Charles V. of Navarre, called the Bad. He granted the privilege of Nobleffe to the Citizens of Paris, which was confirmed by Charles VI. Louis XI. Francis I. and Henry II. but Henry III. reftrained it, in 1557, to the Provoft of the Merchants and the Sheriffs; it was fuppreffed in 1667; reftored in 1707; fuppreffed again in 1715; and at length reftored, in 1716, upon the prefent footing. 1374. An Ordinance to make the Kings of Age at fourteen: under the firft and fecond

Race the Kings were not of age till twenty-two years old.

1380.

Charles VI. twelve Years and nine Months. The Arms of France are reduced to three Flower de Luces. The Order of the Girdle of Hope founded, 1389; and in 1420, by the Treaty of Troyes, it was ftipulated, that Catherine of France fhould be efpoufed to Henry V. of England; upon demife of Charles VI. the Crown fhould devolve to Henry V. of England. From that Treaty to the death of Charles, the Chancellor de Clerk ufed to conclude Letters iffuing from the Court of Chancery, " By the King, and by the Authority of the King of England, Heir and Regent in France."

1422.

Charles VII. twenty Years of Age.

1431.

Henry VI. of England, is crowned King of France in the Church of Notre Dame, at Paris, 17th December. 1453. The taking of Conftantinople, by Mahomet II. puts an end to the Eaftern Empire, which had lafted 1183 Years.

Louis

1461.
Louis XI. thirty-nine Years of Age. 1479. The beginning of the Government of the Czars of Muscovy.

1483.
Charles VIII. aged thirteen Years and two Months.

1498.
Louis XII. called the Father of his People, aged thirty-six Years. 1515. He Married the Princess Mary of England. His Health was then upon the decline; but he forgot his Age to please his Wife. The good King, for the sake of his Wife, had intirely altered his manner of living; for before he used to Dine at eight o'Clock, and now he was obliged to Dine at Noon: He used likewise to go to Bed at six, and now he frequently sat up till midnight.

1515.
Francis I. called the Patron of Learning, Crowned the first of January, aged twenty-one Years. Ignatius Loyola, a Spanish Gentleman, was wounded in 1521, at the Seige of the Castle of Pampelona: He was afterwards the Founder of the Society of Jesuits.

Jesuits. 1529. This Year died Nich. Machiavel. And in 1536 Erasmus died.

1547.

Henry II. aged twenty-nine Years. 1553. Francis Rabelais died. 1558. This year Calais was wrested from the English by the Duke of Guise. At the Peace of Chateau Cambrensis, 1559, the French were to have possession of it for eight Years only, if, during that term, Queen Elizabeth entered into no engagement contrary to the Interest of France or Scotland. But as she broke thro' this Condition, by assisting the Admiral and the Protestants in Scotland, Calais remained in the hands of the French.

1559.

Francis II. at sixteen Years of Age.

1560.

Charles IX. at ten Years of Age. 1562. The Edict of January; being the first that granted Public Exercise of the Protestant Religion. The Parliament refused to register it: *His Verbis, Non Possumus nec debemus.* The first Civil War was occasioned by the Massacre at Vassy: Frederic, Duke

Duke of Guife, is wounded there. The Battle of Dreux, in which the Hugonots are defeated. 1563. Charles is declared of Age by the Parliament of Rouen, at Thirteen and a half Years of Age. Edict of Pacification favourable to the Proteftants. 1564. Catherine de Medicis begins the Buildings of the Tuilleries. 1567. The fecond Civil War. The Battle of St. Dennis, on the 10th, of November; in which the Conftable, Anne de Montmerenci, was mortally wounded: He was feventy-four Years old; yet fought fo manfully that he received eight wounds, and beat out three of the Teeth of James Stewart, a Scotsman, with the Pommel of his Sword. 1568. The fecond Peace was figned at Long Jumeau, called the Short Peace: It lafted but fix Months. The third Civil War was owing to the Queen's defign to feize the Prince of Conde and the Admiral. The German Proteftant Princes join the Hugonots. 1569. The Battle of Jarnac, in which the Catholics were Victorious alfo. The Prince of Conde is killed in cool blood by Montesquieu. On the third of October, the Hugonots were again defeated at Moncontour. The

1570. The third Peace. 1572. The Massacre of the Hugonots at Paris, and divers other parts of the Kingdom, on St. Bartholomew's Day. 1573. The fourth Peace.

1574.

Henry III. aged twenty-three Years. The Prince of Conde and Marshal D'Anville are at the head of the Protestants. 1575. Henry Duke of Guise is wounded in the Face with a pistol shot at the Battle of Chateau Thierry, and from thence called Balafre. Besme, the murderer of Admiral Coligny, is killed by the Hugonots. 1576. The King of Navarre escapes from the Court and joins the Hugonots. A Peace is concluded advantageous to the Hugonots; in which they are allowed the exercise of the pretended Reformed Religion, as it was called in the Edict. Bipartite Chambers are granted to the Reformed, in the eight Parliaments of the Kingdom. The Catholics exasperated at this, occasioned the famous Confederacy, called the Holy League. The Edict is revoked, and the King joins with the Duke of Anjou and the League. 1577. Another Peace concluded. 1578. The Bridge called Pont-Neuf is begun to be Built.

Built. 1579. The King of Navarre has again recourse to Arms. 1580. Peace is brought about by the Duke of Anjou. 1582. an Edict to receive the Gregorian Calendar. 1584. On the Death of the Duke of Anjou, the Duke of Guise is at the head of the League. Henry sends a Deputation to the King of Navarre, now next Heir to the Crown, to change his Religion, that they might act together in Defence of the State. 1585. A Treaty of Peace at Nemours deprives the Protestants of their Privileges: they have recourse to Arms. 1587. The Battle of Courtras in Guienne, in which the King of Navarre gains a Compleat Victory. The Duke de Joyeuse is killed. 1588. The Duke and Cardinal de Guise murdered by order of the King. Catherine de Medicis dies at Blois: advises Henry her Son to be reconciled to the King of Navarre. 1589. Henry III. is Assassinated on the first of August, by Jaques Clement, a Dominican Friar. He declares the King of Navarre his Successor.

1589.

Henry IV. called the Great, aged thirty-six Years. 1590. The Battle of
Ivry,

Ivry, where Henry gains another Victory over the Duke of Mayenne. Death of Pope Sextus Quintus. 1592. Death of Michael de Montagne. 1593. The King makes his Abjuration, and notifies it to all the Parliaments. 1594. The King's Abjuration gives the finishing stroke to the League. Jean Chatel attempts to assassinate the King, but wounds him in the lip only. 1595. He declares War against Spain. The Skirmish of Fontaine Francoise, in which the King, with a small body of Horse, pursues 18,000 Men. Is in great Danger. The Pope grants him Absolution. 1597. The Spaniards surprise the City of Amiens. " Let us go," said Henry, " we have acted the King of France long enough. It is now time to act the King of Navarre." Upon which he besieged and took the Town in Spite of the Arch-duke Albert. 1598. The Edict of Nantes in favour of the Protestants. 1600. Henry marries Mary of Medicis at Lyons. 1603. The Princes of Courtenay produce their Title Deeds, in order to be acknowledged of the Blood Royal, but are disappointed. 1609. A Truce of twelve Years between the Spaniards and the United Provinces; by which the Sovereignty of the Dutch Republic is acknowledged.

1610. The

1610. The King is Aſſaſſinated in his Coach, in which were ſeven others.

1610.

Louis XIII. called the Juſt; born in 1601. 1615. Mary of Medicis begins the Palace of Luxemburg: James de Broſſe, Architect. 1617. The Death of Marſhal D'Anere; which puts an End to the Civil War. 1620. This is the Era of the Diſturbances raiſed by the Hugonots only, without Aſſiſtance from the Catholics. They wanted to new model the Government into a Republic. They had already divided it into eight Circles; the Government of which was to be ſettled on the Lords of their Party: Rohan and Soubize were their Leaders. This Flame was not totally ſubdued 'till 1629; a Year after the Taking of Rochelle. 1624. Richlieu is made a Cardinal. 1627. The poſts of Admiral and Conſtable ſuppreſſed. 1632. Guſtavus Adolphus, King of Sweden, Killed at the Battle of Lutſen. 1641. Mazarine made a Cardinal. 1642. Richlieu dies; and Mazarine is made a Member of the Privy Council the ſame day.

1643.

Louis XIV. aged five Years. The Battle of Rocroy, five Days after the Death of Louis XIII. The Spanish Infantry never Recovered itself since that Defeat. The French were Commanded by the Prince of Conde. 1644. The Title of High and Mighty Lords granted by the King to the States General, in a Treaty at the Hague. 1648. Treaty between Spain and Holland; in which, the former renounces all Right to the United Provinces, and acknowledges them an Independant State. 1651. The King declares his Majority, 7th Sept. 1653. This Year the Intendants of Provinces began to exercise their Authority in the Administration of Justice—the Police and the Revenue: hitherto it had been confined to the Revenue only. 1655. The Tomb of Childeric discovered at Tournay. 1661. Cardinal Mazarine dies, aged fifty-nine. 1669. The King revives the Post of Admiral in favour of the Duke de Vermandois, his natural Son. 1670. The King's Edict enjoining that the profession of a Merchant should not derogate from the honour of the Nobility. 1675. The great Campaign between Turenne and Montecuculli. 1679. Death of of Cardinal de Retz. 1680. Firſt Settlement of the French in the Eaſt Indies, by confirming the acquiſition of Pondicherry in 1674. 1680. Lewis is ſtiled Louis the Great. 1685. Revocation of the Edict of Nantes. 1693. Inſtitution of the Order of St. Louis. 1700. Death of Charles the ſecond, King of Spain. Philip the V. Grandſon of Louis the XIV. is proclaimed King at Madrid. 1701. In this year was formed the Grand Alliance againſt France. The View, in the beginning, was to diſmember as much as they could of the Spaniſh ſucceſſion ; but in the Proſecution of the War, their Succeſſes made them carry their Pretenſions ſo high, as to inſiſt upon the dethroning Philip V. War breaks out in Italy, where Prince Eugene, General for the Emperor, is ſuccefsful againſt De Catinat and Villeroy, and the Duke of Savoy. The League is concluded by the Emperor, King William, and the Dutch. Death of the Duke of Orleans, the King's only Brother, aged ſixty-one. Death of James II. King of England, Aged ſixty-eight. Death of the Duke of Gloceſter ; upon which the Princeſs Sophia, Dutcheſs Dowager of Hanover,

over, is declared to fucceed to the Crown of England after the Death of King William and the Princefs Anne of Denmark. 1702. Death of King William, aged fifty-two. The Emperor, Englifh and Dutch, declare War againft France. 1704. The Archduke Charles, affumes the Title of King of Spain. Lands at Lifbon, affifted by 8,000 Dutch and Englifh Troops, commanded by the Duke of Schomberg. The Duke of Berwick commands the Troops fent by France to the Affiftance of King Philip. Prince of Heffe Darmftadt, after an attempt to fupprize Barcelona, takes Gibraltar. Battle of Hochfted, in which the Duke of Marlbro' gains a complete Victory over the French and Bavarians, commanded by the Elector, Tallard, and De Marfin. The Marfhal de Tallard loft his Son, and is wounded himfelf, and made Prifoner. Twenty-feven Battalions and four Regiments of Dragoons furrender themfelves without making the leaft Defence. 1705. Seige of Gibraltar raifed, which had been attacked by the Spaniards. 1706. The Archduke is proclaimed King at Madrid, 7th June, by Lord Galway. The Battle of Ramillies, the 23d of May; the Elector of Bavaria and the Marfhal de Villeroy com-

mand

mand the French, and the Duke of Marlborough the Allies, who gained a complete Victory. De Villeroy is recalled, and succeeded by Monf. de Vendome, to whom the Duke of Orleans succeeds in Italy. Turin invested by Monf. de la Feuillade. Prince Eugene raises the Seige the seventh of December: the Duke of Orleans is wounded, and De Marsin, loses his Life. Union of England and Scotland. 1707. Battle of Almanza, in which the English and Portuguese are worsted, under the Command of Ruvigny, Earl of Galway, (who had quitted France, on the Revocation of the Edict of Nantes,) and the Marquis de las Minas. The Army of France was commanded by the Duke of Berwick, natural Son of King James II. 1708. Battle of Oudenarde. Seige of Lisle; the Trenches were opened the 22d of August, it surrendered 23d of October, and the Citadel the 8th of December. General Webb being dispatched by the Duke of Marlbro' with 6000 Men to guard a Convoy, is attacked by De la Motte with 20000 Men : he defeated De la Motte, and arrives safe with the Convoy. The English seize the Islands of Sardinia and Minorca. 1709 Battle of Malplaquet, in Favor of the English and Allies.

lies. Battle of Pultowa, in which the King of Sweden was totally defeated by the Ruffians. 1710. Death of the Dauphin, aged fifty Years. The Archduke is made Emperor upon the death of the Emperor Joseph. Preliminaries for a Peace signed at London, in October: Chief Articles, that Louis should acknowledge the Queen of Great Britain, and the Succession to the Crown in favour of the House of Hanover; that just and reasonable Measures should be taken to prevent the Crowns of France and Spain from being United under the same Prince; that the Dutch should have a Barrier against France; that the Empire and Austria should also have a sure and proper Barrier; and, that the Fortifications of Dunkirk should be demolished upon the Conclusion of the Peace. 1712. Opening of the Congress of Utrecht. Suspension of Arms, agreed to by France, Spain, and England, is prolonged. The King of Spain renounces the Crown of France, for himself and his Descendants. 1713. Peace signed at Utrecht. Gibraltar and Minorca Ceded for ever to Great-Britain. 1715. On the first of September, died Louis XIV.

KINGS OF FRANCE *since the Year* 1000.

1000. Robert.	1316. Philip 5.
1031. Henry.	22. Charles 4.
60. Philip.	28. Philip 6.
1108. Louis 6.	50. John.
37. Louis 7.	64. Charles 5.
80. Philip 2.	80. Charles 6.
1223. Louis 8.	1422. Charles 7.
26. Louis 9.	31. Henry.
70. Philip 3.	61. Louis 11.
85. Philip 4.	83. Charles 8.
1314. Louis 10.	98. Louis 12.
	1515. Francis.
	47. Henry 2.
	59. Francis 2.
	60. Charles 9.
	74. Henry 3.
	89. Henry 4.
	1610. Louis 13.
	43. Louis 14.
	1715. Louis 15.
	1774. Louis 16.

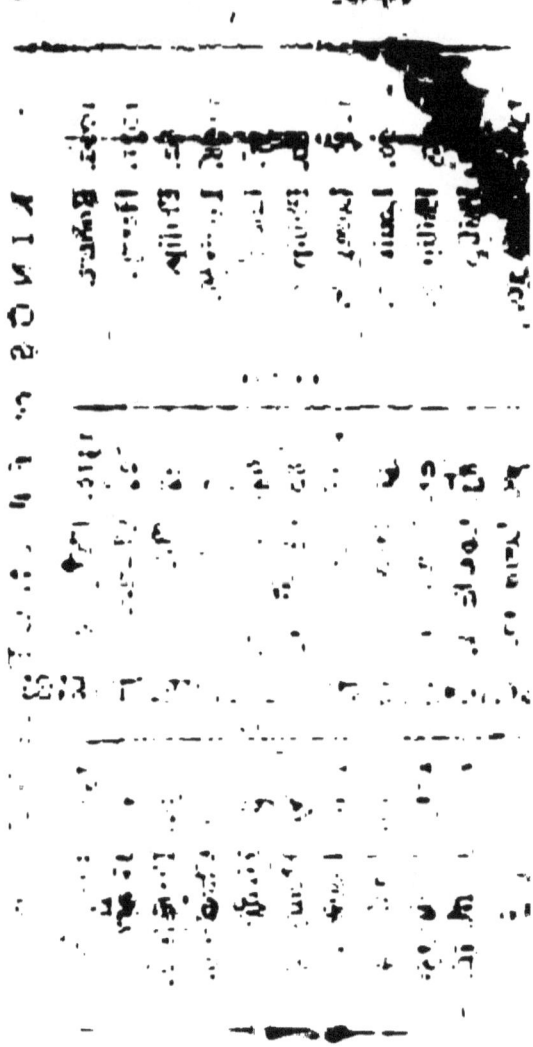

ABSTRACT

OF THE

FIRST VOLUME

OF

BLACKSTONE's COMMENTARIES

ON THE

LAWS OF ENGLAND.

ADVERTISEMENT.

THE Study of the Law has a found so terrific to such as have no views to make it a profession, that it has deterred many, even from peeping into it. Sir William Blackstone has, however, done his part so clearly, and in a style as familiar as was possible, so that no man can be disgusted.

The first Volume is, in its various parts, so frequently the Subject of common Conversation, that it is almost a reproach not to be acquainted with it. The Author made the following Abstract many years ago, and from its use to himself, he ventures to offer it to Public Notice.

ABSTRACT

OF THE

FIRST VOLUME

OF

BLACKSTONE's COMMENTARIES

ON THE LAWS OF ENGLAND.

THE municipal law of England, or the rule of civil conduct prescribed to the inhabitants of this kingdom may be divided into two kinds; the *lex non scripta*, the unwritten or common law; and *lex scripta*, the written or statute law.

The *lex non scripta*, includes not only *general customs*, or the common law, so called; but also the *particular customs* of certain parts of the kingdom; and likewise those *particular laws* that are by custom observed only in certain courts and jurisdictions.

I. As to general customs, or the common law, properly so called; this is that law, by which proceedings and determinations in
the

the king's ordinary court of juſtice are guided and directed. This, for the moſt part, ſettles the courſe in which lands deſcend by inheritance; the manner and forms of acquiring and transferring property; the ſolemnities and obligations of contracts: the rules of expounding wills, deeds, and acts of parliament; the reſpective remedies of civil injuries; the ſeveral ſpecies of temporal offences, with the manner and degree of puniſhment; and an infinity of minuter particles, which diffuſe themſelves as extenſively as the ordinary diſtribution of common juſtice requires. Thus, for example, that there ſhall be four ſuperior courts of record, the chancery, the king's bench, the common pleas, and the exchequer;—that the eldeſt ſon alone is heir to his anceſtor;—that property may be acquired and transferred by writing;—that a deed is of no validity unleſs ſealed;—that wills ſhall be conſtrued more favourable and deeds more ſtrictly;—that money lent upon bond is recoverable by action of debt;—that breaking the public peace is an offence, and puniſhable by fine and impriſonment;—all theſe are doctrines that are not ſet down or written in any ſtatute or ordinance,

ordinance, but depend upon immemorial usage, that is, upon common law, for their support.

The judges, in the several courts of justice, are the depositaries of the laws; the living oracles, who must decide in all cases of doubt, and who are bound by an oath to decide according to the law of the land. But as the judgments themselves, and all proceedings previous thereto, are carefully registered and preserved, under the name of *records*, in reference to them it is an established rule to abide by former precedents, where the same points come again in litigation.

II. The second branch of the unwritten laws of England, are particular customs, or laws which affect only the inhabitants of particular districts.

To make a particular custom good, the following are necessary requisites.

1. That it have been used so long, that the memory of man runneth not to the contrary. So that if any one can shew the beginning of it, it is no good custom. For which reason no custom can prevail against an express

prefs act of parliament; since the ftatute itfelf is a proof of a time when fuch a cuftom did not exift.

2. It muft have *continued*. Any interruption would caufe a temporary ceafing the revival gives it a new beginning, which will be within time of memory, and thereupon the cuftom will be void. But this muft be underftood with regard to an interruption of the *right*, for an interruption of the poffion only for ten or twenty years will not deftroy the cuftom. As if I have a right of way by cuftom over another's field, the cuftom is not deftroyed, though I do not pafs over it for ten years; it only becomes more difficult to prove: but if the *right* be any how difcontinued for a day, the cuftom is quite at an end.

3. It muft have been *peaceable* and acquiefced in. For as cuftoms owe their original to common confent, their being immemorially difputed, either at law or otherwife, is a proof that fuch confent was wanting.

4. Cuftoms muft be *reafonable*; or rather, taken negatively, they muft not be unreafonable. Upon which account a cuftom may be

be good, though the particular reason cannot be assigned; for it sufficeth, if no legal reason can be found against it. Thus a custom in a parish, that no man shall put his beasts into the common till the 3d of October, would be good; and yet it would be hard to shew the reason why this day in particular is fixed upon, rather than the day before or after. But a custom that no cattle shall be put in till the lord of the manor has first put in his, is unreasonable, and therefore bad : for peradventure the lord will never put in his ; and then the tenants will lose all their profits.

5. Customs ought to be *certain*. A custom, that lands shall descend to the most worthy of the owner's blood, is void; for how shall this worth be determined ? But a custom to descend to the next male of the blood, exclusive of females, is certain, and therefore good. A custom, to pay two-pence per acre in lieu of tythe is good ; but to pay sometimes two-pence, and sometimes three-pence, as the occupier of the land pleases, is not good for its uncertainty. Yet a custom, to pay a year's improved value for a fine on a copyhold estate, is good : though the value is

a thing uncertain. For the value may at any time be ascertained; and the maxim of the law is, *Id certum est, quod certum reddi potest.*

6. Customs, though established by consent, must be (when established) *compulsory*; and not left to the option of every man, whether he will use them or not. Therefore a custom, that all the inhabitants shall be rated towards the maintenance of a bridge shall be good; but a custom, that every man shall contribute thereto at his own pleasure, is idle and absurd, and, indeed, no custom at all.

7. Lastly, customs must be *consistent* with each other: one custom cannot be set up in opposition to another. For if both are really customs, then both are of equal antiquity and both established by mutual consent; which to say of contradictory customs is absurd.

III. The third branch of them are those particular laws, which by custom are adopted and used only in certain peculiar courts, and jurisdictions. And by these are understood the civil and canon laws. These are termed *leges non scriptae*: they do not bind the

the people of England, though we have laws with that title which do; but becaufe they are the materials of foreign jurisdiction, which cannot bind a Britifh fubject.

There are four fpecies of courts in which the civil and canon laws are permitted under different reftrictions to be ufed.

1. The courts of the arch-bifhops and bifhops and their derivative officers, ufually called in our law courts chriftian, *curiae chriftianitatis*, or the ecclefiaftical courts. 2. The military courts. 3. The courts of admiralty. 4. The courts of the two univerfities.

I. The courts of common law have the fuperintendency over thefe courts; to keep them within their jurifdictions, to determine wherein they exceed them, to reftrain and prohibit fuch excefs, and (in cafe of contumacy) to punifh the officer who executes, and in fome cafes the judge who enforces, the fentence fo declared to be illegal.

II. The common law has referved to itfelf

self the expofition of all fuch acts of parliament, as concern either the extent of thefe courts, or the matters depending before them.

III. An appeal lies from all thefe courts to the king, in the laft refort; which proves that the jurifdiction exercifed in them is derived from the crown of England, and not from any foreign potentate, or intrinfic authority of their own.

The civil and canon laws, though admitted in fome cafes by fome courts, are only fubordinate laws, *leges fub graviori lege*; and are but inferior branches of the cuftomary or unwritten laws of England, properly called, the king's ecclefiaftical, the king's military, king's maritime, or the king's academical, laws.

Let us next proceed to the *leges fcriptae*, the written laws of the kingdom, which are ftatutes, acts, or edicts, made by the king's majefty by and with the advice and confent of parliament. The oldeft of thefe now extant, is the famous Magna Charta as confirmed in parliament*. Statutes are either *general* or *fpecial*, *public* or *private*.

* 9 Hen. III.

OF THE

COUNTRIES

SUBJECT TO THE

LAWS OF ENGLAND.

THE kingdom of England, over which our municipal laws have jurisdiction, includes not, by the common law, either Wales, Scotland, or Ireland, or any other part of the king's territories. And yet the civil laws and local customs of this territory do obtain, in part or in all, with more or less restrictions, in these and many other adjacent countries. Wales first by a statute 27 Hen. VIII, and by the statute 34 and 35 of the same, chap. 26, is divided into shires, &c. and is made to differ very little from England.

England, and that only in the nature of privileges, and immaterial peculiarities, such as are to be found in many counties in England.

Scotland has its own municipal laws, they have been in a few instances altered by parliament, but so little, that they may be said to have their full force; and the common law of England is, generally speaking, of no force or validity in Scotland.

The town of Berwick, though subject to the crown ever since the conquest of it in the reign of Edw. IV, is not part of this kingdom, nor subject to the common law. By statute*, where England only is mentioned in the act, the same shall notwithstanding be deemed to comprehend the dominion of Wales and town of Berwick upon Tweed. The general law used there is the Scots law, and the ordinary process of the courts of Westminster-hall is there of no authority.

Ireland is still a distinct kingdom, though a dependent subordinate kingdom; therefore it must necessarily conform to, and be obliged

* 20 Geo. II. chap. 42.

by

by such laws as the superior state thinks proper to prescribe *.

Our American plantations may be looked at in the same light; though distinct, they are dependent dominions, and though the common law has no authority there, yet they are subject to control of parliament: but (like Scotland, and Isle of Man) not bound, unless particularly named. It is particularly declared by statute†, that all laws, by-laws, usages, and customs, which shall be in practice in any of the plantations, repugnant to any law, made or to be made in this kingdom relative to the said plantations, shall be utterly void and of none effect. The Islands of Man, Jersey, Guernsey, Sark, and Alderney, are governed by their own laws. The king's writ is of no effect; but his commission is.

Three counties, Chester, Durham, and Lancaster, are called counties palatine. The two former by prescription, or immemorial custom; the latter was created by Edward III, in favour of Henry Plantagenet,

* 6 Geo. I. chap. 5.

† 7 & 8 Will. III. chap. 22.

firſt earl and then duke of Lancaſter. Counties palatine are ſo called *a palatio*; becauſe the owners thereof, had there *jura regalia*, as fully as the king hath in his palace; *regalem poteſtatem in omnibus*. They might pardon treaſons, murders and felonies; they appointed all judges and juſtices of the peace; all writs and indictments ran in their name, and all offences are ſaid to be done againſt their peace, and not, as in other places, *contra pacem domini regis*. Theſe palatine privileges were in all probability originally granted to the counties of Cheſter and Durham, becauſe they bordered upon enemies countries, Wales and Scotland; in order that the owners, being encouraged by ſo large an authority, might be the more watchful in it's defence; and that the inhabitants, having juſtice adminiſtered at home, might not be obliged to go out of the county, and leave it open to the enemies incurſion. There were formerly two others, Pembrokeſhire and Hexham, the latter ſince united to Northumberland: but theſe were aboliſhed by parliament*, and the powers before mentioned of the others were abridged, though ſtill all writs are witneſſed in their name, and all

---

* 27 Hen. VIII. 14 Eliz.

forfeitures

forfeitures for treason by the common law accrue to them. The county of Durham is the only one now remaining in the hands of a subject.

Chester was united to the crown by Henry III, and gives title of earl to the king's eldest son. Lancaster was vested in Henry VII, and his heirs.

The isle of Ely is not a county palatine, though erroneously so called; but only a royal franchise; the bishop having, by grant of king Henry I. *jura regalia*, within the isle of Ely, and thereby he exercises jurisdiction over all causes, as well criminal, as civil.

There are also counties *corporate*; where the officers of the county have no power to intermeddle: such as London, York, &c. These have been granted by the special favour and grace of the kings of England.

OF THE
RIGHTS
OF
PERSONS.

Of the absolute Rights of Individuals.

THE rights defined by the several statutes, consist in a number of private immunities; which will appear indeed to be no other, than the *residuum* of natural liberty, which is not required by the laws of society to be sacrificed to public convenience; or else those civil privileges, which society has engaged to provide, in lieu of those natural liberties given up by individuals. These therefore were formerly, either by inheritance or purchafe, the rights of all mankind ; but, in moft countries in the world being now more or lefs debafed and deftroyed, they at prefent may be faid to remain, in a peculiar and emphatical manner, the rights of the people of England. And thefe are reducible to three principal or primary articles.

The right of perfonal fecurity. The right of perfonal liberty. The right of private property.

1. The right of perfonal fecurity confifts, in a perfon's legal and uninterrupted enjoyment of his life, his limbs, his body, his health, and his reputation.

2. Next to perfonal fecurity, the law of England afferts and preferves the perfonal liberty of individuals. This confifts in the power of loco-motion, of changing fituation, or removing one's perfon to whatfoever place one's own inclination may direct; without imprifonment or reftraint, unlefs by due courfe of law. If reftrained by any decree, he may have a writ of *Habeas Corpus*, to bring his body before the court of king's bench or common pleas.

The parliament, whenever it fees occafion, can authorize the crown, by fufpending the *Habeas Corpus* act for a fhort and limited time, to imprifon fufpected perfons without giving any reafon for fo doing.

The king may iffue out his *ne exeat regnum*, to prohibit any of his fubjects from going into foreign parts. This may be neceffary for the public fervice. But no power on earth, except the authority of a parliament, can fend any fubject *out of* the land againft his will; no not even a criminal. For exile, or tranfportation, is a punifhment unknown to the common law; and, wherever it is now inflicted, it is either by the choice of the criminal himfelf, to efcape a capital punifhment, or elfe by the exprefs direction of fome modern act of parliament. By the *Habeas Corpus* act*, no fubject of this realm, who is an inhabitant of England and Wales, or Berwick, fhall be fent prifoner into Scotland, Ireland, Jerfey, Guernfey, or places beyond the feas; under very high fines and penalties.

And though the king may command the

* 31 Cha. II. chap. 2.

attendance

attendance of all his liege-men *within* the realm, yet he cannot fend any man *out of* the kingdom, even on the public fervice : he cannot even conftitute a man lord deputy or lieutenant of Ireland, nor make him a foreign embaffador againft his will.

III. The third abfolute right, inherent in an Englifhman, is that of property: which confifts in the free ufe, enjoyment, and difpofal of all his acquifitions, without any control or dimunition, fave only by the laws of the land.

The barriers which ferve to protect and maintain inviolate thefe three great and primary rights, are,

1. The conftitution, powers, and privileges of parliament.

2. The limitation of the king's prerogative, by bounds fo certain and notorious, that it is impoffible he fhould exceed them without the confent of the people.

3. A third fubordinate right of every Englifhman is that of applying to the courts of juftice for redrefs of injuries. The emphatical words of Magna Carta, fpoken in the

perfon

person of the king, who in the judgment of law, (says Sir Edward Coke) is ever present and repeating them in all his courts, are, "*nulli vendemus, nulli negabimus, aut differemus rectum vel justitiam:* and every subject therefore" continues the same learned author, "for injury done him *in bonis, in terris, vel persona,* by any other subject, be he ecclesiastical or temporal without any exception, may take his remedy by the course of the law, and have justice and right for the injury done to him, freely without sale, fully without any denial, and speedily without delay."

4. If the ordinary course of law is too defective to reach any uncommon injury or infringements of the rights before mentioned, there is a power of every individual of petitioning the king, or either house of parliament, for the redress of grievances. No petition can be signed by more than twenty persons, unless approved of by three justices of the peace or the major part of the grand jury, of the county; and in London by the lord mayor, aldermen, and common council; nor shall any petition be presented by more than ten persons at a time*.

The

---

* 1 W. & M. stat. 2, chap. 2.

5. The fifth and laſt auxiliary right of the ſubject is, that of having arms for their defence, ſuitable to their condition and degree, and ſuch as are allowed by law. Which is alſo allowed by the laſt mentioned ſtatute; and is indeed a public allowance, under due reſtrictions, of the natural right of reſiſtance and ſelf-preſervation, when the ſanction of ſociety and laws are found inſufficient, to reſtrain the violence of oppreſſion. Esto perpetua!

OF THE

PARLIAMENT.

I. AS to the manner and time of affembling. The parliament is regularly to be fummoned by the king's writ or letter, iffued out of chancery by the advice of the privy council, at leaft forty days before it begins to fit. On the demife of a king or queen, if there be then no parliament in being, the laft parliament revives, and is to fit again for fix months, unlefs diffolved by the fucceffor. A new parliament fhall be called within three years after the determination of the former.†

II. The conftituent parts of a parliament are

† 6 W & M. chap. 2.

are the king's majefty, fitting there in his royal political capacity, and the three eftates of the realm; the lords fpiritual, the lords temporal, (who fit, together with the king, in one houfe) and the commons, who fit by themfelves in another. And thefe form the great corporation or body politic of the kingdom, of which the king is faid to be *caput, principium, et finis.* For upon their coming together the king meets them, either in perfon or by reprefentation; without which there can be no beginning of a parliament; and he alfo has alone the power of diffolving them.

Of the houfe of peers, there are fome who fit by defcent, as all antient peers; fome by creation, as do all new-made peers; and fome by election, which is the cafe of the fixteen, who reprefent the body of the Scots nobility.

The number of the houfe of commons is 513, and of the Scots 45; in all 558. And every member, though chofe by one particular diftrict, when elected ferves for the whole realm. For the end of his coming there is not particular, but general; not barely to advantage his conftituents, but the *common*-wealth: to advife his majefty (as

Vol. I. O o appears

appears by the writ of summons) *de communi confilio fuper negotiis, quibufdam arduis et urgentibus, regem, ftatum et defenfionem regni Angliae et ecclefiae Anglicanae concernentibus.* And therefore he is not bound, like a deputy in the united provinces, to confult with, or take advice of his conftituents upon any particular point, unlefs he himfelf thinks it proper fo to do.

III. The parliament is the place where that defpotic power which muft in all governments refide fomewhere, is entrufted by the conftitution of this kingdom. It has fovereign and uncontrolable power over all laws and over all matters, under whatever denomination, ecclefiaftical, or temporal, civil, military, maritime or criminal. All mifchiefs and grievances, that tranfcend the ordinary courfe of law, are within the reach of this tribunal. It can regulate or new model the fucceffion to the crown; as was done in the reign of Henry VIII. and William III. It can alter the eftablifhed religion of the land; as was done in many inftances, in the reigns of Henry VIII. and his three children. It can change and create afrefh even the conftitution of the kingdom and of parliaments

ments themfelves; as was done by the act of union, and the feveral ftatutes for triennial and feptennial parliaments. It can, in fhort, do every thing that is not naturally impoffible. The whole of the law and cuftom of parliament has it's original from this one maxim; "that whatever matter arifes con-
" cerning either houfe of parliament, ought
" to be examined, difcuffed, and adjudged,
" in that houfe to which it relates, and not
" elfewhere."

The *privileges* of parliament are indefinite; fome however of the moft notorious, are, privilege of fpeech, of perfons, of their domeftics, and of their lands and goods. This includes as well illegal violence, as alfo legal arrefts, and feizures by procefs from the courts of law. Thefe privileges however, endure no longer than the feffion of parliament, fave only as to the freedom of his perfon: which in a peer is for ever facred and inviolable; and in a commoner for forty days after every prorogation, and forty days before the next appointed meeting; but this holds not in fuch crimes

as

as treason, felony, or breach of the peace.*

* House of Commons.

In the reign of Henry the third, Monfort earl of Leicester summoned a parliament in London, and besides the barons of his own party, and several ecclesiastics, he ordered returns of two knights from every shire, and deputies from the boroughs.

	Returning places.	Members.
In the reign of Henry VII.	147	296.
Henry VIII. added	32	38.
Edward VI.	22	24.
Mary	12	22.
Elizabeth	31	62.
James I. before	14	27.
By authority of parliaments before the union		44.
By the act of union		45.
	258.	558.

The triennial act was from the 6th of William III. to 1716, George I.

OF

OF THE

KING, and his TITLE.

I. WITH regard to his title. The grand fundamental maxim upon which the *jus coronae*, or right of succession to the throne of these kingdoms, depends, is, that the crown is, by common law and constitutional custom, hereditary; and this in a manner peculiar to itself: but the right of inheritance may from time to time be changed or limited by act of parliament; under which limitations the crown shall continue hereditary.

II. Of his royal family. The first and most considerable branch of which, regarded by the laws of England, is the queen. The queen is a public person, exempt and distinct from the king; and not, like other married women, so closely connected as to have lost all legal or feperate exiftence fo long as the marriage continues. She can make leafes, grant copyholds, &c. without her lord's concurrence. The reafon given by Sir Edward Coke is, the common law fuppofes the king's continual care and ftudy is for the public, and *circa ardua regni,* and therefore he may not be troubled or difquieted on account of his wife's domeftic concerns; and therefore it vefts in the queen a power of tranfacting her concerns without the intervention of the king, as if fhe was an unmarried woman. It is equally treafon to compafs or imagine the queen's death, as of the king himfelf: and to defile, or violate the queen confort, amounts to the fame crime; as well in the perfon committing the fact, as in herfelf.* But it is not high treafon to confpire her death or defile her when queen dowager; for this reafon, becaufe the fucceffion to the crown is not thereby endangered. Yet, *pro dignitate regali,* no man can marry a queen dowager without fpecial licence from the king, on pain of forfeiture of his lands and goods; but if married fhe does not lofe her regal dignity, as dowager peereffes do their peerage when they marry commoners.

* 25 Edw. III.

The prince of Wales, or heir apparent to the crown, and alfo his royal confort, and the princefs royal, or eldeft daughter of the king, are likewife peculiarly regarded by the laws; and to confpire their death, or to violate them, is high treafon, equally as if of the king or queen. In 1718, upon a queftion referred to all the judges by king George I. it was refolved by the opinion of ten againft two, that the education and care of all the king's grandchildren while minors, and the care and approbation of their marriages, when grown up, did belong of right to his majefty, as king of this realm, during their father's life.

III. Of his councils. The firft of thefe is the high court of Parliament. Secondly, the peers of the realm are by their birth hereditary counfellors of the crown, and may be called together by the king to impart their advice in all matters of importance to the realm, in time of parliament, or not; and in the law books it is laid down, that peers are created for two reafons; 1. *Ad confulendum.* 2. *Ad defendendum regem*: wherefore they have their high privileges, becaufe the law intends, that they are always affifting the king with their counfel for the
good

good of the common-wealth; or keeping the king and realm in safety by their prowess and valour.

A third council belonging to the king, according to Sir Edward Coke, are, the judges of the courts of law, for law matters. but the principal council belonging to the king is his privy council, by way of eminence called The council. The king's will is the sole constituent of a privy counsellor.

OF THE

KING's PREROGATIVE.

I. THE law afcribes to the king the attribute of *fovereignty* or preeminence. *Rex et vicarius*, fays Bracton, *et minifter Dei in terra: omnis quidem fub eo eft, et ipfe fub nullo, nifi tantum fub Deo.* He is faid to have *imperial* dignity. His realm is declared an *empire* by feveral acts of parliament.* The meaning of the legiflature, in the ufe of thefe words, is, that the king is equally fovereign and independent within thefe his dominions, as any emperor is in his empire; and owes no kind of fubjection to any other potentate upon earth.

As to private injuries; if any perfon has,

* 24 Hen. VIII. chap. 12. 25 Hen. VIII. chap. 28.

in point of property, a juſt demand upon the king, he muſt petition him in the court of chancery, where his chancellor will adminiſter right as matter of grace, though not upon compulſion. "And if a prince "ſhould permit a ſubject to bring an action "againſt him in one of his own courts, the "end of ſuch action is not to compel the "prince, but to perſuade him."* In caſes of ordinary public oppreſſion, where the vitals of the conſtitution are not attacked, the law has alſo aſſigned a remedy. For, as a king cannot uſe his power illegally, without the advice of evil counſellors, and the aſſiſtance of wicked miniſters, theſe men may be examined and puniſhed, by means of indictments, and parliamentary impeachments, that no man ſhall dare to aſſiſt the crown in contradiction to the laws of the land. But it is at the ſame time a maxim in thoſe laws, that the king himſelf can do no wrong; ſince it would be a great weakneſs and abſurdity in any ſyſtem of poſitive law, to define any poſſible wrong, without any poſſible redreſs: for, if the law could ſuppoſe this, it would veſt a ſuperior coercive authority in ſome other hand to correct

* Puffendorf.

it:

it: for the suppofition of the law is, that neither the king nor either houfe of parliament (collectively taken) is capable of doing any wrong; fince in fuch cafes the law feels itfelf incapable of furnifhing any adequate remedy.

II. Befides the attribute of fovereignty, the law alfo afcribes to the king, in his political capacity, abfolute *perfection*. The king can do no wrong. Which is to be underftood, firft, that whatever is exceptionable in the conduct of public affairs is not to be imputed to the king, nor is he anfwerable for it perfonally to the people: for this doctrine would totally deftroy that conftitutional independence of the crown, which is neceffary for the ballance of power, in our free, active, and therefore compounded, conftitution. And, fecondly, it means that the prerogative of the crown extends not to do any injury: It is created for the benefit of the people, and therefore cannot be exerted to their prejudice. The king is moreover, not only incapable of *doing* wrong, but even of *thinking* wrong: for the law will not caft that imputation on that magiftrate whom it entrufts with the

the executive power, as if he was capable of intentionally difregarding his truft: but attributes to mere impofition thofe little inadvertencies, which if charged on the will of the prince, might leffen him in the eyes of his fubjects.

III. Another attribute of the king's majefty is his *perpetuity*. The king never dies. For immediately upon his deceafe, his imperial dignity, without any *interregnum* or interval, is vefted at once in his heir; who is, *eo inftanti*, king to all intents and purpofes. And fo tender is the law of fuppofing even a poffibility of his death, that his natural diffolution is called his *demife*; *dimiffio regis, vel coronae:* an expreffion that fignifies merely a transfer of property. The king has the fole power of fending abroad and receiving embaffadors from foreign countries; of making treaties, leagues, and alliances with foreign ftates; for thefe could never be done by the people in a collective body. He has the power alfo of making war and peace for the fame reafon; but in the tranfactions above cited, if conducted to the detriment of, and are inglorious to the nation, minifters sters might be brought to a very severe account. These are the principal prerogatives of the king, respecting the nation's intercourse with foreign nations; in all which he is considered as the delegate or representative of the people. But in domestic affairs he is considered

I. As a constituent part of the supreme legislative power; and, as such, has the prerogative of rejecting such provisions in parliament, as he judges improper to be passed.

II. As generalissimo, or the first in military command, within the kingdom; and this extends not only to all fleets and armies, but even to all forts, and other places of strength: and no subject, according to Sir Edward Coke, can build a castle, or house of strength imbattled, without the licence of the king.

III. He is as the fountain of justice and conservator of the peace of the kingdom: and hence it is, that all juridictions of courts are either mediately or immediately derived from the crown, their proceedings run generally in the king's name, they pass under

under his feal, and are executed by his officers. All offences are either againſt the king's peace, his crown, or dignity; and are ſo laid in every indictment. For, as the public, (an inviſible body,) has delegated all its power and rights, with regard to the execution of the laws, to one viſible magiſtrate, all affronts to that power, and breaches of thoſe rights, are immediatly offences againſt him, to whom they are ſo delegated by the public. He is therefore the proper perſon to proſecute. And hence ariſes another prerogative, the power of *pardoning ;* for it is reaſonable that he who is injured ſhould have the power of forgiving. His majeſty, in the eye of the law, is always preſent in all his courts, though he cannot perſonally diſtribute juſtice. His judges are the mirror by which the king's image is reflected. It is the regal office, and not the royal perſon, that is always preſent in court, and always ready to undertake proſecutions, or pronounce judgment, for the benefit and protection of the ſubject.

IV. The king is likewiſe the fountain of honour, of office, and of privilege: and this in a different fenfe from that wherein he is ftiled the fountain of juftice; for here he is the parent of them. It is impoffible that government can be fupported without due fubordination of rank; that the people may know and diftinguifh fuch as are fet over them, in order to yield them their due refpect and obedience; and alfo that the officers themfelves, being encouraged by emulation and the hopes of fuperiority, may the better difcharge their functions: and the law fuppofes, that no one can be fo good a judge of their feveral merits as the king himfelf, who employs them. It has therefore intrufted with him the fole power of conferring dignities and honours, in confidence that he will beftow them on none, but fuch as deferve them. And as he has the power of conferring honours, fo he has of conferring offices, privileges to particular perfons, place or precedence to any of his fubjects, and converting aliens into denizens; whereby fome very particular privileges of naturalborn fubjects are conferred on them.

V. Another light in which the laws confider the king in, is the arbiter of commerce, fo far as relates to domeftic concerns. The eftablifhment of public marts, markets

and

and fairs, is in him. The limitation of thefe public reforts, to fuch time and fuch place as may be moſt convenient for the neighbourhood, forms a part of oeconomics, or domeſtic polity; which, confidering the kingdom as a large family, and the king as the maſter of it, he clearly has a right to difpofe and order as he pleafes. Secondly, the regulation of weights and meafures. Thirdly, as money is the medium of commerce, it is the king's prerogative, as arbiter of domeſtic commerce, to make it current and give it authority. The coining of money is in all ſtates the act of the king. The impreſſion or ſtamping is his undoubted prerogative, as is the denomination of, and the current value of the coin; but his prerogative feemeth not to extend to the debafing or enhancing of the value of the coin, above or below the ſterling value.* He may legitimate foreign coin, and make it current by declaring at what value it ſhall be taken in payments: at prefent we have no fuch legitimated money; Portugal coin being only current by private confent. The king may alfo at any time decry, or cry down, any coin of the kingdom, and make it no longer current.

* 25 Edw. III. chap. 13.

VI. The king is, lastly, considered by the laws, as the head and supreme governor of the national church. In virtue of this authority the king convenes, prorogues, restrains, regulates, and dissolves all eclesiastical synods or convocations: and this was an inherent prerogative in the crown, long before Henry VIII.* and so in the opinion of many lawyers and historians, and so vouched by Sir Edward Coke. The houses of convocation resemble the houses of lords and commons. This constitution is said to be owing to the policy of Edward I. who, by these means, let in the inferior clergy to the privilege of forming ecclesiastical canons, (which before they had not) and also introduced a method of taxing ecclesiastical benefices, by consent of convocation.

As head of the church, the king's right arises to the nomination to vacant bishopricks, and certain other ecclesiastical preferments. As such also, he is the *dernier resort* in all ecclesiastical causes, an appeal lying ultimately to him in chancery from the sentence of every ecclesiastical judge†.

* 8 Hen. VI. chap. 1.
† 25 Hen. VIII. chap. 9.

OF THE

KING's REVENUE.

I. THE king has the custody of the temporalties of bishops; by which are meant all the lay revenues, lands, (in which is included his barony) which belong to an archbishop or bishop's fee: and these upon a vacancy are immediately the right of the king, as a consequence of his prerogative. Another reason why the policy of the law has vested them in the king, is, because as the successor is not known, the lands, &c. of the fee might be liable to spoil and devestation. By keeping the fee vacant, and making the bishops pay for their temporalties, some of the kings have raised large sums; but now they are transmitted to the successor with all
profits

profits accruing, from the time of the vacancy, &c.

II. The king is entitled to a corody, as the law calls it, out of every bishoprick: that is, to send one of his chaplains to be maintained by the bishop, or to have a pension from him 'till he promotes him to a benefice: and though now fallen into total disuse, Sir Matthew Hale says, 'tis due of common right and that no prescription will discharge it.

III The king is entitled to all the tythes arising in extraparochial places, thro' an implied trust, that he will distribute them for the good of the clergy in general.

IV. The next branch consists in the firstfruits, and tenths of all spiritual preferments in the kingdom: but this is now employed for the benefit of the clergy.

V. The rents and profits of the demesne lands of the crown, *terrae dominicales regis;* and which though they formerly consisted of divers rich manors, and lordships, are now almost entirely granted away to private subjects. But after king William III. had been

been so very liberal, an act* was made, whereby all future leases or grants from the crown for a longer time than thirty-one years or three lives are declared null and void: except with regard to houses, which may be for fifty years. And no reversionary lease can be made, but to fill up the remaining term of the last. The misfortune is, the act was made too late.

VI. Profits arising from military tenures, purveyance, and pre-emption. This was a right in the king of buying up provisions and other necessaries at an appraised valuation, without consent of the owner. These were productive of many mischiefs to the people, and were given up by king Charles II. and the parliament, in part of recompence, settled on him, and his heirs for ever, the hereditary excise of fifteen-pence per barrel on all beer and ale sold in the kingdom, and a proportionable sum on all other liquors.

VII. The rents payable by such persons as are licensed by the crown to sell wine by re-

---

* 1. Ann. stat. 1. chap. 11.

tail throughout the kingdom, except in a few privileged places. Thefe were firft fettled by ftatute* to make up with the beer excife the equivalent to the rights given up as before mentioned; but were abolifhed fince,† and 7000l. *per annum*, iffuing out of the new ftamp duties impofed on wine licences, was fettled on the crown.

VIII. The profits arifing from the king's forefts, which confifted principally in amercements or fines levied for offences againft the forefts-laws; but as few, if any courts of this fort has been held fince 1632, 8 Cha. I. nobody would wifh to fee a revival of them.

IX. The profits arifing from the king's ordinary courts of juftice. Thefe were of various kinds; but, in procefs of time, have been almoft all granted away, or applied to particular purpofes: fo that, though the law-fuits are loaded with them, very little returns into the king's exchequer; for a part of whofe royal maintenance they were in-

* 12 Cha. II. chap. 25.

† 30 Geo. II. chap. 19.

tended.

tended. All future grants of them are* to endure no longer than the prince's life who grants them.

X. The right to *royal fish*, which are whale and sturgeon, when either thrown on shore, or caught near the coast, are the king's property, in consideration of his guarding and protecting the seas from pirates and robbers.

XI. Another maritime revenue, and founded on the same reason, is that of shipwrecks; which are also declared to be so by statute,† and were so long before at common law. Wreck, by common law, was where any ship was lost at sea, and the goods or cargo were thrown upon the land; and these were adjudged to the king: for it was held, by the loss of the ship, all property was gone out of the original owner. But the rigour of this law, has from time to time been softened in favour of the distressed proprietors; and now it consists only in that rational part, where, if no owner can be ascertained, it belongs to

* 1. Ann. stat. 2. chap. 7.

† 17. Edward II. chap. 11.

the

the king. It is the bufinefs of the fheriff to take care of thefe; where the revenue is not granted out to lords of manors, as a royal franchife. It is to be obferved that to conftitute a legal *wreck*, the goods muft come to land. If they continue at fea, the law diftinguifhes them by the barbarous appellations of *jetfam*, *flotfam*, and *ligan*. The firft is where goods are caft into the fea and fink: the fecond, where they continue fwimming on the waves: the laft, where they are funk, but have a buoy or cork faftened to them, in order to be found. Thefe three do not pafs in a king's grant of wrecks to any man; thefe like the other wrecks, are alfo given to the legal owner, if he can be found; and by feveral late acts, all poffible care is taken by the legiflature, to render the lofs as fmall as may be to the fufferer.

XII. The right to mines, which has it's original from the king's prerogative of coinage, in order to fupply him with materials: and therefore the mines, properly royal, are filver and gold. By the old common law, if filver or gold were found in mines of bafe metal, the whole was the king's:

but

but it is now settled, that the king, or persons claiming royal mines under his authority, may have the ore, paying a certain price as stated in the act.*

XIII. To the same original, in part, may be referred the revenue of treasure-trove, called in Latin *thesaurus inventus*, which is where any coin, bullion, plate, gold, or silver, is found and the owner unknown, it belongs to the king: but if it is found in the sea, or upon the earth, it is the finders, no owner appearing. A man that hides his treasure, does not mean to abandon it; but reserves a right of claiming it whenever he sees occasion; but if he dies and the secret with him, the law gives it the king, as a part of his royal revenue. But if a man scatters his treasure in the sea, or upon the earth, he is construed to have absolutely abandoned his property, and returned it into the common stock, without any intention of reclaiming it; therefore it belongs, as in a state of nature, to the first occupant or finder; unless the owner appears and asserts his right, which then proves the loss was by accident, and not with an intent to renounce his property. Formerly all treasure-trove belonged

1 W. & M. stat. 1. chap. 30,—5. chap. 6.

to the finder; as was alfo the cafe of the civil law. When the feudal laws obtained in England, it was death to conceal treafure-trove from the king; now only fine and imprifonment.

XIV. Waifs, *bona waviata*, are goods ftolen, and thrown away by the thief in his flight, for fear of being apprehended. Thefe are given to the king as a punifhment to the owner for not himfelf purfuing the felon, and taking away his goods from him. And therefore if the party robbed do his diligence to follow and apprehend the thief, or do convict him afterwards, he fhall have his goods again. Waived goods do not belong to the king, unlefs feized by fomebody for his ufe; and if the party can feize them firft, though at the diftance of twenty years, the king fhall never have them. The goods of a foreign merchant in fuch a cafe, fhall never be waifs; as well for the encouragement of commerce, as that there cannot be a wilful default in the foreigner's not purfuing the thief, he being fuppofed a ftranger to our laws, ufages, and cuftoms, and language.

XV. Eftrays are fuch valuable animals as are

are found wandering in any manor or lordſhip, and no man knoweth the right owner of them; in which caſe the law gives them to the king as lord paramount of the ſoil, in recompence for the damage they may have done therein; and they now moſt commonly belong to the lord of the manor, by ſpecial grant from the king. They muſt be proclaimed in the church and two market towns next adjoining to the place where found, and muſt be kept a year and a day; and then, if no owner appears, they belong to the king or his grantee without redemption. But if a lord keepeth an eſtray three quarters of a year, and within the year it ſtrayeth again, and another lord gets it, the firſt lord cannot take it again. Any beaſt may be an eſtray, that is by nature tame and reclaimable, and in which there is a valuable property. A ſwan may alſo be an eſtray, but no other fowl. Cattle and ſwans being of a reclaimed nature, the owner's property in them is not loſt merely by their temporary eſcape; and they are alſo a ſufficient pledge for the lord of the franchiſe for keeping them a year and a day. For he that takes an eſtray is bound to find it in proviſions ſo long as he keeps it, and free from damage, and may not uſe it by way of labour,

but

but is liable to an action for so doing. Yet he milks a cow, or the like, for this tends to the preservation of the animal. Besides the particular reasons before given why the king should have the several revenues of royal fish, wrecks, treasure-trove, waifs, and estrays, there is also this general reason, that they are *bona vacantia*, or goods in which no one else can claim a property. And therefore by the way of nature, they belong to the first occupant or finder; but, in settling most of the modern governments in Europe, it was thought proper (to prevent that strife and contention, which the mere title of occupancy was apt to create and continue, and to provide for the support of public authority in a manner least burdensome to individuals) that these rights should be annexed to the supreme power by the positive laws of the state. And so it came to pass, as Bracton expresses it, *haec quae nullius in bonis sunt, et olim fuerunt inventoris de jure naturali, jam efficiuntur principis de jure gentium.*

XVI. Forfeitures of lands and goods for offences; *bona confiscata*, so called by the Civilians, because they belonged to the *fiscus* or imperial treasury. The true reason and only

only substantial ground of any forfeiture for crimes consists in this; that all property is derived from society, being one of those civil rights which are conferred upon individuals, in exchange for that degree of natural freedom, which every man must sacrifice when he enters into civil and social communities. If therefore a member of any national community violates the fundamental contract of this association, by transgressing the municipal law, he forfeits his right to such privileges as he claims by such contract; and the state may very justly assume that portion of property, which the laws have assigned him. Hence, in crimes of an atrocious nature the laws have sometimes a total confiscation of the moveables or personal estate; and in many cases a perpetual, and in others only a temporary, loss of the offender's immoveable or landed property; and have vested them both in the king, who is the person supposed to be offended, being the one visible magistrate in whom the majesty of the public resides.

Deodand is a species of forfeiture, a part of the *censsus regalis*, arising from the misfortune rather than the crime of the owner.

By

By this is meant whatever perfonal chattel is the immediate occafion of the death of any reafonable creature; which is forfeited to the king, for pious ufes, and diftributed in alms by his high almoner: but it feems originally to have been given to the church, for an expiation for the fouls of fuch as were fnatched away by fudden death. So the apparel of a ftranger found dead was applied to purchafe maffes for the good of his foul. And this may account for that rule of the law, that where an infant falls from a cart, or the like, not being in motion, and is killed, there is no forfeiture; whereas, if the cart is in motion, and it falls from thence, it is certainly forfeited. And whether adult or infant, if the cart, ox, or horfe be in motion, they fhall in either cafe be a deodand; *omnia quae ad mortem movent funt Deo danda*, fays Bracton. Where a thing, not in motion, is the immediate occafion of a man's death, that part only is forfeited, which was the caufe; thus, if a man be climbing up a wheel, and is killed by falling from it, the wheel alone is a deodand: but, where the thing is in motion, not only that part which immediately gives the wound, (as the wheel, which runs over the body) but all things which

move

move with it and help to make the wound more dangerous, (as the cart and lading, which increase the pressure of the wheel) are forfeited. For if a man kills another with my sword, the sword is forfeited as an accursed thing. And therefore, in all indictments for homicide, the instrument of death and the value are presented and found by the grand jury, (as, that the stroke was given with a certain penknife, of the value of sixpence) that the king or his grantee may claim the deodand: for it is no deodand, unless it be presented as such by a jury of twelve men. No deodands are due from accidents on the high seas, that being out of the jurisdiction of the common law: but if a man falls from a boat or ship in fresh water, and is drowned, the vessel and cargo, in strictness, are a deodand.

XVII. Escheats of lands, which happen upon the defect of heirs to succeed to the inheritance; whereupon they in general revert to and vest in the king, who is esteemed, in the eye of the law, the original proprietor of all the lands in the kingdom.

XVIII. The last branch of the king's ordinary revenue, consists in the custody of idiots.

idiots. An idiot, or natural fool, is one that hath no underſtanding from his nativity; and is therefore by law preſumed never to have any. The cuſtody of the idiot, and his lands were formerly veſted in the lord of the fee, (and ſtill, by ſpecial cuſtom, in ſome manors, the lord ſhall have the ordering of idiot and lunatic copyholders) but, by the manifold abuſes of this power by ſubjects, it was provided by common conſent, that it ſhould be given to the king*, as common conſervator of his people, in order to prevent the idiot from waſting his eſtate. The king ſhall have ward of the lands of natural fools, taking the profits without waſte or deſtruction, and ſhall find them neceſſaries; and after the death of ſuch idiots he ſhall render the eſtate to the heirs; in order to hinder ſuch idiots from aliening their lands, and their heirs from being diſinherited. A man is not an idiot, if he has any glimmering of reaſon, ſo that he can tell his age, parents, and the like common matters. But he who is born deaf, dumb, and blind, is looked upon by the law as in the ſtate of an idiot. A lunatic, or *non compos mentis*, is one who hath had underſtanding, but

* 17 Edward II. chap. 9.

by

by accident, fuch as ficknefs, grief, and the like, has loft it. A lunatic is properly one that hath lucid intervals. To thefe the king is alfo guardian, but to a different purpofe: for the law always imagines, that thefe accidental misfortunes may be removed; and therefore only conftitute the crown a truftee to protect their property, and to account to them for all profits received, if they recover, or after their deceafe to their reprefentatives. The lord chancellor, by fpecial authority from the king, is entrufted with the cuftody of idiots, and lunatics. The next heir can never be appointed the committee or guardian of the perfon lunatic, becaufe it is his intereft that the party fhould die. But, the fame objection lays not againft his being manager of the eftate, becaufe it is clearly his intereft, by good management, to keep it in condition; accountable however to the court of chancery, and to the *non compos*, if he recovers; or otherwife, to his adminiftrators. The next of kin, if not his heir, may be committee to the perfon of the lunatic; for his intereft is in the life of the lunatic; that the perfonal eftate, which may come to him or his heirs, may be increafed by the favings. Laws a-
gainft

against spendthrifts and prodigals, do not exist in England, as in some other countries, for they hardly seem calculated for the genius of a free nation, who claim and exercise the liberty of using their own property as they please. "*Sic utere tuo, ut alienum non laedas,*" is the only restriction our laws have given with regard to oeconomical prudence. And the frequent circulation and transfer of lands, and other property, which cannot be effected without extravagance somewhere, are perhaps not a little conducive towards keeping our mixed constitution in due health and vigour.

OF THE

KING'S

EXTRAORDINARY REVENUE.

THE king's *extraordinary* revenue confifts of annual taxes.

I. The land tax; which at four fhillings in the pound brings in two millions.

II. The malt tax.

The perpetual taxes are,

I. The cuftoms; or the duties, toll, or tariff, payable upon merchandize exported and imported. The confiderations upon which the moft part of this revenue was invefted in the king, antiently, was, 1. That he gave the

the fubject leave to depart the country with his goods, &c. 2. Becaufe the king was bound of common right to keep up the ports and havens, and protect the merchant from pirates.

II. The excife duty.

III. The duty upon falt.

IV. The poft-office, or duty for carriage of letters.

V. The ftamp duties.

VI. The duty upon houfes and windows.

VII. The duty paid by hackney coaches and chairs.

VIII. The duty upon offices and penfions; confifting in the payment of one fhilling in the pound (over and above all other duties) out of all falaries, fees, and perquifites, of offices and penfions payable by the crown. This was impofed by ftatute,* and is under the direction of the commiffioners of the land tax. Since which, many others are added, that would be tedious to recount.

* 31 Geo. II. chap. 22.

OF

SUBORDINATE MAGISTRATES.

THE sheriff is an officer of great antiquity, his name being derived from two Saxon words, shire reeve, the bailiff or officer of the shire. He is called in Latin, *vice-comes*, as being the deputy of the earl or *comes*; to whom the custody of the shire was committed: but now he does all the king's business independent of the earl; the king by his letters patent committing *custodiam comitatus* to the sheriff, and him alone. Sheriffs were formerly* chosen by the inhabitants of the county, where it was not hereditary. The people, or *incolae territorii*, chose twelve electors, and they nominated three persons, *ex quibus rex unum confirmabat*. This was the

* 28 Edw. I. chap. 8.

old

old Gothic method; but thefe popular elections creating tumults, was put an end to by ftatute,* which enacted, that the fheriffs, fhould from thenceforth be affigned by the chancellor, treafurer, and judges. But now the cuftom is, that all the judges, and certain other great officers meet in the exchequer chamber on the morrow of St. Martin, and nominate three, one of which the king appoints. In his judicial capacity he is to hear and determine all caufes of forty fhillings value in his county court; he decides likewife the election of knights of the fhire, of coroners and verdurers, and to judge of the qualifications of voters. As keeper of the king's peace, both by common law and fpecial commiffion, he is the firft man of the county, and fuperior in rank to any nobleman therein, during his office. He may apprehend, and commit to prifon, all perfons who break or attempt to break the peace. He may, and is bound *ex officio*, to purfue and take all traitors, murderers, felons and other misdoers, and commit them to gaol for fafe cuftody; and to perform this, or in defence of the county againft the king's enemies if they land, he may command all the people of his coun-

* 9 Edw. II. ftat. 2.

ty to attend him; which is called the *poffe comitatus*: which fummons every perfon under the degree of a peer, above fifteen years old, is obliged to attend upon warning, under pain of fine and imprifonment. But he may not act as an ordinary juftice of the peace, or try any criminal offehce. In his minifterial capacity he is bound to execute all procefs from the king's courts of juftice: to ferve the writ, arreft, and take bail; fummon and return the jury for tryal, and muft fee the judgement of the court carried into excution, though it extends to death itfelf. It is his bufinefs to preferve the rights of the king, within his bailiwic. He muft feize to the king's ufe all efcheats, fines, and forfeitures; and keep all waifs, wrecks, eftrays and the like, and muft alfo collect the king's rents if commanded by procefs from the exchequer. To execute thefe various offices, he has many inferior officers; an under-fheriff, bailiffs, and goalers; who muft neither buy, fell, nor farm their offices, on forfeiture of 500l.

The under-fheriff ufually performs all the duties of the office; except where the perfonal

nal prefence of the high-fheriff is neceffary. But no under-fheriff fhall abide in his office above one year, and if he does,* he fhall forfeit 200l. And no under-fheriff or fheriff's officer fhall practice as an attorney, during the time he continues in fuch office: for this would be a great inlet to partiality and oppreffion.

Bailiffs, are either of the hundred, or fpecial. Thofe of the hundreds are appointed by the fheriffs to collect the fines therein; to fummon the juries; to attend the judge and juftices at the affizes, and quarter feffions; and alfo to execute writs and procefs. But thefe men not being generally thoroughly fkilful in the latter branch of their office, it is ufual to join fpecial bailiffs with them; who are generally mean perfons fo employed for their adroitnefs in feizing their prey. The fheriff being anfwerable for the mifdemeanors of thefe bailiffs, they are ufually bound in a bond for the due execution of their office, and thence called bound-bailiffs, which the

* 23. Hen. VI. chap. 8.

common people have corrupted into a much more homely appellation.

Goalers are also servants of the sheriff, and he must be responsible for their conduct; if they suffer any to escape that are committed by lawful warrant, the sheriff shall answer it to the king, if a criminal matter; or, in a civil case, to the party injured. And to this end the sheriff must have lands sufficient to answer the king and his people. The vast expence that custom had introduced in the serving this office was restrained by statute*, that the sheriffs should keep no table but for his own family, nor give presents to the judge or his servants, and that he should not have more than forty men in livery; yet, for the sake of decency, he may not have less than twenty in England, nor twelve in Wales; upon forfeiture, in any of these cases, of 200l.

II. The coroner is also a very ancient office at the common law. He is called coroner, *coronator*, because he hath principally to do with common pleas of the crown, or

---

* 13 & 14 Cha. II. chap. 21.

such

such wherein the king is more immediately concerned. And in this light the lord chief justice of the king's bench is the principal coroner in the kingdom, and may execute that office in any part of the realm. This officer is of equal antiquity with the sheriff; and ordained together with him to keep the peace, when the earls gave up the wardship of the counties. They are chosen by the freeholders of the county court: formerly none but lawful and discreet knights could be chosen, and there was an instance* of a man's being removed from this office, being only a merchant. The coroner is chosen for life: he may be removed by being sheriff or verdurer; and by a late statute†, for extortion, neglect, or other misbehaviour. His office and power is chiefly judicial, and this, in great measure ascertained by statute, ‡ *de officio coronatoris*; and consists, first, in inquiring concerning the manner of the death of any person slain, or who dies suddenly. And this must be done *super visum corporis*; for, if the body be not found, the

* 5. Edw. III.
† 25. Geo. II. chap. 29.
‡ 4. Edw. I.

Vol. I.   T t   coroner

coroner cannot fit: for he muſt fit at the very place where the death happened; and his enquiry is made by a jury from four, five, or fix of the neighbouring towns, over whom he is to prefide. If any be found guilty by this inqueſt of murder, he is to commit him to prifon for further trial, and is alfo to enquire concerning their lands, goods and chattels, which are forfeited thereby: but, whether it be murder or not, he is to enquire whether any deodand has accrued to the king, or the lord of the franchife, by this death: and muſt certify the whole of this inquifition to the court of king's bench, or next affizes. Another branch of his office is concerning wrecks; and to certify whether wrecks or not, and who is in poffeffion of the goods; and fo of treafure-trove.

His miniſterial office is only as the ſheriff's fubſtitute. For when juſt exception can be taken to the ſheriff, for fufpicion of partiality, the procefs muſt then be awarded to the coroner, inſtead of the ſheriff, for execution of the king's writs.

III. Juſtices of the peace; the principal of whom is the *cuſtos rotulorum*. The king's majeſty is by his office and dignity royal, the firſt

first conservator of the peace within all his dominions; and may give authority to any other to see the peace kept, and to punish such as break it: hence it is usually called the king's peace. The lord chancellor or keeper, the lord treasurer, the lord high steward of England, the lord mareschal, and the lord high constable (when any such officers are in being) and all the justices of the court of king's bench (by virtue of their offices) and the master of the rolls (by prescription) are general conservators of the peace throughout the whole kingdom, and may commit all breakers of it or bind them in recognizance to keep it: the other judges are only so in their own courts. The coroner and sheriff are both so in their country; and may take a security for the peace. Constables and tything-men, and the like, are conservators of the peace within their own jurisdictions; and may apprehend all breakers of the peace, and commit them 'till they find sureties for the keeping it. Those that were without any office, simply, and merely conservators of the peace, were chosen by the freeholders at the county court, *de probioribus et melioribus in comitatu suo in custodes pacis.* This form was first altered,

tered, when Isabel, queen of Edward II. had contrived to depose her husband and set up her son, by a false resignatation of the father. Being a thing without example, it was feared it would much alarm the people; especially as the old king was living, though hurried about from castle to castle; till at last he met with an untimely death. To prevent therefore any risings, the new king sent writs to all the sheriffs, commanding that the peace be kept throughout his bailiwic, on pain and penalty of disinheritance and the loss of life and limb. And a short time after it was ordained in parliament, that, good and lawful men should be assigned, in each county, to keep the peace; and this assignment to be by the king's commission. And in this manner, and upon this occasion, was the election of the conservators of the peace taken from the people, and given to the king. But still they were called only conservators, wardens, or keepers of the peace, till by statute,* they had a power of trying felonies; and then they acquired the more honourable appellation of justices. The qualifications for serving in this office have been differently fixed; it now stands, that

* 34 Edw. I. chap. 1.

every

every juftice, except as is therein excepted, fhall have 100l. *per annum* clear of all deductions†; and, if he acts without his qualification, he fhall forfeit 100l. and of this qualification the juftice fhall make oath. No practifing attorney, folicitor, or proctor, fhall be capable of acting as a juftice of the peace. As the office is conferred by the king, fo it fubfifts only during his pleafure, and is determinable, 1. By the demife of the crown. 2. By exprefs writ under the great feal, difcharging any particular perfon from being juftice. 3. By fuperfeding the commiffion by writ of *fuperfedeas*, which fufpends the power of all juftices, but does not totally deftroy it; feeing it may be revived by another writ, called a *procedendo* 4. By a new commiffion, which virtually, though filently, difcharges all the former juftices that are not included therein. 5. By acceffion to the office of fheriff or coroner. The power, office, and duty of a juftice of the peace, is now of fuch extent, that few care to undertake, and fewer underftand, the office. Several ftatutes have

† 5. Geo. II. chap. 11.

been

been made to protect the undesigned slip of a well meaning justice. But, on the other hand, any malicious or tyrannical abuse of their office is sure to be punished severely; and all persons who recover a verdict against a justice, for any wilful or malicious injury, are intitled to double costs.

IV. Of constables. Constables derived their office from that very high one of lord high constable, which has been disused in England, except on particular occasions, since the attainder of Stafford duke of Buckingham, in Henry 8th's time; and about a century after disused in France. His office was to regulate all matters of chivalry, and by the statute of Westminster, two constables in every hundred and franchise shall inspect all matters relating to arms and armour.

Constables are of two sorts, high and petty. Their duty, is to keep the king's peace in their several districts; and to that purpose they are armed with very large powers of arresting, imprisoning, breaking open houses, and the like. One of their principal duties, arising from the statute of Westminster, which

which appoints them, is to keep watch and ward in their jurisdictions.

Ward is chiefly intended of the day time, for the apprehending rioters, and highway-robbers. Watch is properly applicable to night only.

V. Surveyors of the highways. Every parish is bound of common right to keep the high roads, that go through it, in good repair; unless by reason of the tenure of lands, or otherwise, the care is consigned to a private person. By our antient laws, no man's estate was free from this, being a part of the *trinoda necessitas*; viz. *expeditio contra hostem, arcium constructio, et pontium reparatio*. Surveyors were appointed by statute*, and were fixed upon by the constables and churchwardens; but now they are constituted by two justices of the peace, out of substantial inhabitants having 10l. *per annum* of their own, or renting 30l. *per annum*, or are worth in personal estate 100l.

VI. Overseers of the poor. The poor of England, till the time of Henry VIII. sub-

* 2 & 3. Ph. & M. chap. 8.

sisted

sifted entirely upon private benevolence. For, though it appears by common law, the poor were to be sustained by parsons, rectors of the church, and parishioners; so that none of them die from default of sustenance; and though by statute†, the poor are directed to be sustained in the cities or towns wherein they were born, or dwelt three years (which seems to be the first rudiments of parish settlements) yet till another statute, ‡ no compulsory methods were chalked out for this purpose. The monasteries, in particular, were their principal resource. Upon their dissolution abundance of statutes were made in the reign of Henry VIII. but not effectual; and it was not till Elizabeth had tried many fruitless experiments, that overseers of the poor were appointed.* The two great objects of this statute seem, 1. To relieve the impotent poor, and them only. And, 2. To find employment for such as were able to work.

† 12 R. II. chap. 7.—19 Hen. VII. chap. 12.

‡ 27. Hen. VIII. chap 26.

* 43. Eliz. chap. 2.

OF

OF THE

PEOPLE

WHETHER

ALIENS, DENIZENS, OR NATIVES.

THE firſt and moſt obvious diviſion of the people is into aliens and natural-born ſubjects. The latter are ſuch as are born within the dominions of the crown of England, that is, within the ligeance, or as more generally, the allegience of the king; and aliens, ſuch as are born out of it. Allegiance is that tye, or *ligamen,* that binds the ſubject to the king, in return for that protection which the king affords the ſubject.

The oath of allegiance, which was administered for upwards of 600 years, contained "a promise to be true and faithful to the king and his heirs, and truth and faith to bear of life and limb and terrene honour, and not to know or hear of any ill or damage intended him, without defending him therefrom." But, at the revolution, the terms of this oath were altered, the subject only promising "that he will be faithful and bear *true* allegiance to the king." But the law holds that there is an implied, original, and virtual allegiance, owing from every subject to his sovereign, antecedently to any express promise; and although the subject never swore any faithful allegiance in form. An alien born may purchase lands, or other estates: but not for his own use; for the king is thereupon entitled to them. Children of aliens, born here, are, generally speaking, natural-born subjects: in France it is otherwise. A denizen is an alien born, but who has obtained *ex donatione regis* letters patent to make him an English subject: an high and incommunicable branch of the royal prerogative. A denizen is a kind of middle state. He may take lands by purchase or devise, which an alien may not; but cannot

not take by inheritance: for his parent, through whom he muſt claim, being an alien, had no inheritable blood, and could not therefore convey any to the ſon. The iſſue of a denizen, *before* denization, cannot inherit to him; but his iſſue born *after* may. A denizen is not excuſed from paying the alien's duty, and ſome other mercantile burthens. No alien, or denizen, or perſon naturalized, can be a member of the privy council, or parliament, or have any office of truſt, civil or military, or be capable of any grant from the crown. By naturalization, an alien is put exactly in the ſame ſtate as if he had been born in the king's ligeance; except the aforementioned exceptions, and this can be changed only by act of parliament. He muſt have received the ſacrament one month before the bringing in of the bill, and muſt take the oaths of allegiance and ſupremacy before the parliament. Every foreign ſeaman who ſerves two years on board an Engliſh ſhip is *ipſo facto* naturalized; and all foreign proteſtants, and jews, upon their reſiding ſeven years in any of the American colonies, without being abſent above two months at a time, are upon taking the oaths naturalized to all intents and purpoſes.

Of

OF THE

CLERGY.

DURING the attendance on divine service a clergyman is privileged from arrests in civil suits. In cases of felony, a clerk in orders shall have the benefit of his clergy, without being branded in the hand; and may have it more than once. He cannot sit in the house of commons; nor take any lands or tenements to farm, upon pain of 10l. *per* month, and total avoidance of the lease; nor can he engage in any manner of trade, nor sell any merchandize, under forfeiture of the treble value.

An arch-bishop or bishop is elected by the chapter of his cathedral church, by virtue

tue of a licence from the crown, termed a *conge d'elire*; and, if the dean and chapter delay their nomination twelve days, the nomination shall devolve to the king. This election or nomination if of a bishop, must be signified by the king's letters patent to the arch-bishop of the province; if it be of an arch-bishop, to the other arch-bishop and two bishops, or to four bishops; requiring them to confirm, invest, and confecrate the person so elected. The bishop elect shall sue to the king for his temporalties, shall make oath to the king and none other, and shall take restitution out of the king's hands only. And if such dean and chapter do not elect in the manner by this act appointed, or if such arch-bishop or bishop do refuse to confirm, invest, and confecrate such bishop elect, they shall incur all the penalties of a *praemunire*. An arch-bishop is the chief of the clergy in a whole province; and has the inspection of the bishops, as well as of the inferior clergy, and may deprive them on notorious cause. He has also his own diocese wherein he exercises episcopal jurisdiction; as in his province he exercises archiepiscopal. He cannot call the bishops and clergy in his province to

meet

meet in convocation, without the king's writ. During the vacancy of any fee, he is guardian of the fpiritualties, as the king is of the temporalties; and he executes all ecclefiaftical jurifdiction therein. If an archiepifcopal fee be vacant, the dean and chapter are the guardians of the fpiritualties, fince the office of prior of Canterbury was abolifhed at the reformation. The arch-bifhop is entitled to prefent by lapfe to all livings in the difpofal of his diocefan bifhops, if not filled within fix months. And he has a cuftomary prerogative, when a bifhop is confecrated by him, to name a clerk or chaplain of his to be provided for by fuch fuffragan bifhop. It is now ufual for fuch bifhop to make over by deed to the arch-bifhop, his executors or affigns, the next prefentation of fuch dignity or benefice in the bifhop's difpofal within that fee, as the arch-bifhop fhall choofe; which is therefore called his option: which options are not binding to the fucceffors of the bifhop. This was an encroachment of the pope on the imperial prerogative called *primae* or *primariae preces*. He has alfo by ftatute*, the power of granting difpenfa-

* 25. Hen. VIII. chap. 21.

tions

tions in any cafe, not contrary to the holy
fcriptures and the law of God, where the
pope formerly ufed them: which is the
foundation of his granting licences, to marry
at any place or time, to hold two livings,
and of conferring degrees, in prejudice of the
two univerfities. If a bifhop refigns, it
muft be to his metropolitan; but an arch-
bifhop to the king only.

A dean and chapter are the council of the
bifhop, to affift him in all temporal and fpiritual concerns of his fee. All antient deans,
are elected by the chapter by *conge d'elire,*
and letters miffive of recommendation: but
in thofe chapters, founded by Henry VIII.
out of the fpoils of the diffolved monafte-
ries, the inftallation is merely by the king's
letters patent. Till a certain ftatute* was
made, the bifhop's grant or leafe would not
have bound his fucceffors, unlefs confirmed by the dean and chapter. If any
fpiritual perfon be made a bifhop, all the
preferments he was before poffeffed of are void;
and the king may prefent to them by his
prerogative royal. But they are not void by
the election, but by the confecration.

* 32 Hen. VIII. chap. 28.

A parfon

A parson *persona ecclesiae*, is one that hath full possession of all the rights of a parochial church. He is called parson, *persona*, because by his person the church, which is an invisible body, is represented; and he is in himself a body corporate, in order to protect and defend the rights of the church (which he personates) by a perpetual succession. He is sometimes called the rector, or governor, of the church: but the appellation of *parson*, (however it may be depreciated by familiar, clownish, and indiscriminate use) is the most legal, most beneficial, and most honourable title that a parish priest can enjoy; because such a person, (Sir Edward Coke observes) and he only, is said *vicem seu personam ecclesiae gerere*. A parson has, during his life, the freehold in himself of the parsonage house, the glebe, the tithes and other dues; but these are sometimes *appropriated*. At the first establishment of parochial clergy, the tithes of the parish were distributed in a fourfold division; one for the use of the bishop, another for maintaining the fabric of the church, a third for the poor, and a fourth for the incumbent. When the sees of bishops were more amply endowed, the division was into

three

three parts only. And hence it was inferred by the monaſtics, that a ſmall part was ſufficient for the officiating prieſt, and that the remainder might well be applied to the uſe of their own fraternities, (the endowment of which was conſtrued a work of the moſt exalted piety) ſubject to the burden of repairing the church and providing for it's conſtant ſupply. And therefore they begged and bought all advowſons within their reach, and then appropriated the benefices to the uſe of their own corporations. At the diſſolution of the monaſteries by ſtatute*, the appropriations of the ſeveral parſonages, which belonged to thoſe reſpective religious houſes, (amounting to more than one third of all the pariſhes) would have been by the rules of the common law diſappropriated; had not a clauſe in thoſe ſtatutes intervened, to give them to the king in as ample a manner as the abbots, &c. formerly held them. Theſe appropriating corporations, or religious houſes, were wont to depute one of their own body to perform the religious duties in thoſe pariſhes of which the ſociety was thus the parſon. This vicegerent of the appropriator was called *vicarius*, or *vicar*. The abuſes from this were

* 27 Hen. VIII. chap. 28—31 Hen. VIII. chap. 13.

so flagrant, that by statute in Richard II. and lastly by statute 4 Henry IV. chap. 12. it is ordained, that the vicar shall be a secular person, and not a member of any religious house; that he shall be perpetual, not removeable at the caprice of the monastery; and that he shall be canonically instituted and inducted, and be sufficiently endowed, at the discretion of the ordinary, for these three express purposes; to do divine service, to inform the people, and keep hospitality. There are four requisites necessary to the becoming a parson or vicar; holy orders, presentation, institution, and induction. If any person obtains orders, or a licence to preach by money or corrupt practices (which seems to be the true, though not the common notion of simony) the person giving such orders forfeits 40l. and the person receiving 10l. and is incapable of holding any ecclesiastical preferment for seven years afterwards.

A bishop may refuse a presentation from the patron of the advowson of the church. 1. If the patron is excommunicated, and remains in contempt forty days. Or, 2. If the clerk be a bastard, an outlaw, an excommunicate, an alien, or under age. Next with regard to his faith or morals; as for any particular heresy,

herefy, or vice that is *malum in se*: but if the bifhop only alleges in general, that he is *fchifmaticus inveteratus*, or objects a fault that is *malum prohibitum* only, fuch as haunting taverns, playing at unlawful games, and the like, it is not good caufe of refufal. Or, the clerk may be unfit for want of learning, or other matter of ecclefiaftical cognizance, there the bifhop muft give notice to the patron of fuch his caufe of refufal, who, being generally a layman, is not fuppofed to have knowledge of it; elfe he cannot prefent by lapfe: but if the caufe be temporal, he is not bound to give notice. When a vicar is inftituted, he, (befides the ufual forms) takes, if required by the bifhop, an oath of perpetual refidence, for the maxim of the law is, *vicarius non habet vicarium*: for as the non-refidence of the appropriator was the caufe of the perpetual eftablifhment of vicarages, the law judges it very improper for them to defeat the end of their conftitution: efpecially as, if any profits are to arife from putting in a curate, and living at a diftance from the parifh, the appropriator, who is the real parfon, has the elder title to them. When the ordinary is alfo the patron and *confers* the living, the prefentation and inftitution

stitution are one and the same act, and called a collation to a benefice. Upon institution, a clerk may enter on the parsonage house and glebe, and take the tythes; but cannot grant or let them, or bring any action for them, till induction. Induction is performed by mandate from the bishop to the archdeacon. It is done by giving the clerk corporal possession of the church, by holding the ring of the door, tolling a bell, or the like; and is a form required by law, with intent to give all the parishioners due notice, and sufficient certainty of their new minister, to whom their tythes are to be paid. 'Tis therefore the investiture of the temporal part of the benefice, as institution is of the spiritual: and when a clerk is thus presented, instituted, and inducted into a rectory, he is then, and not before, in full and compleat possession, and is called in law *persona impersonata*, or parson *imparsonée*. By statute*, persons absenting themselves from their benefice for one month together, or two months in the year, incur a penalty of 5l. to the king, and 5l. to any person that will sue for the same: except chaplains to the king, or others therein mentioned. Legal residence is not only in the parish, but also in the par-

* 21 Hen. VIII. chap. 13.

sonage

sonage house : for it hath been resolved, that the statute intended residence, not only for serving the cure, and for hospitality ; but also for maintaining the house, that the successor may also keep hospitality there. A clerk may be deprived of his benefice, among other reasons, for absenting himself sixty days in one year from a benefice belonging to a popish patron, to which he was presented by either of the two Universities. If any rector or vicar nominates a curate to the ordinary to be licenced, the ordinary shall settle his stipend under his hand and seal, not exceeding 50l. nor under 20l. *per annum*, and on failure of payment may sequester the profits of the benefice.

O F

OF THE

CIVIL STATE.

THE civil state confifts of the nobility and commonalty. The degrees of nobility now in ufe are dukes, marquiffes, earls, vifcounts, and barons. The right of peerage feems to have been originally territorial; that is, annexed to lands, caftles, manors, &c. and might be alienated with thofe lands, &c. 'Tis thus the bifhops fit in the houfe of lords in right of fucceffion to certain ancient baronies annexed, or fuppofed to be annexed, to their epifcopal lands. The caftle of Arundel, in 11 Henry VI. was adjudged to confer an earldom on it's poffeffor; but when alienations grew fo frequent, the dignity of peerage was confined to the lineage of the party ty ennobled, and no longer became territorial. Peers are now created either by writ or patent: for thofe who claim by prefcription muft fuppofe either a writ or a patent; though by length of time it is loft. Creation by writ has this advantage over that by patent, that he holds the dignity to him and his heirs, without any words to that purpofe in the writ; whereas in letters patent there muft be words to direct the inheritance. A nobleman, in criminal cafes, fhall be tried by his peers. The great are always obnoxious to envy of the people: they ought not therefore to be judged by the people; befides it would be robbing them of the privilege of the meaneft fubjects, that of being tried by their equals, which is fecured to all the realm by *magna charta*, chap. 29. It is faid, it does not extend to bifhops; who, though lords of parliament, and fit there by virtue of their baronies which they hold *jure ecclefiae*, yet are not ennobled in blood, and confequently not peers with the nobility. Peereffes either in their own right, or by marriage, fhall be tried by the fame judicature as peers of the realm. If a woman, noble in her own right, marries a commoner, fhe ftill remains noble, and fhall be tried by her peers: but if fhe be only

only noble by marriage, and by a second marriage is allied to a commoner, she loses her dignity; for as by marriage it is gained, by marriage it is also lost. Yet if a dutchess dowager marries a baron, she continues a dutchess; for all nobility are *pares* and therefore it is no degredation. A peer, sitting in judgment, gives his verdict upon his honour: and gives answers to bills in chancery upon his honour; but, when he is examined as a witness, he must be sworn: for the respect, which the law shews to the honour of a peer, does not extend so far as to overturn a settled maxim, *in judicio non creditur nisi juratis.* A peer cannot lose his nobility, but by death or attainder; though there was once an instance, in the reign of Edward IV. of the degredation of George Nevile duke of Bedford by act of parliament, on account of his poverty, which rendered him unable to support his dignity. The commonalty, tho' divisible into degrees, yet are all in law, peers in respect of their want of nobility. The first name of dignity, next beneath a peer, was anciently that of *vidame, vice domini,* or *valvasors*: mentioned by ancient lawyers as *viri magnae dignitatis*; but their original office is forgot. The first dignity after the nobility, is *knight*
of

of the order of St. George, or *of the garter*; first instituted by Edward III. 1344. *Knights banneret*, if created in the field by the king, he ranks next barons: else he ranks after *baronets*, who are the next order. Then comes *knights of the bath*; instituted by Henry IV, and revived by George the first. The last are *knights bachelors*; the most ancient, though the lowest, rank: for we have an instance of king Alfred conferring this order on his son Athelstan. A knight's fee amounted, in Henry the second's time, to 20l. *per annum*; and every one such was obliged to be knighted, and attend the king in his wars, or fine for his non-compliance. These, says Sir Edward Coke, are all the names of *dignity* in this kingdom, esquires and gentlemen being only names of *worship*. But before these the herald ranks all colonels, serjeants at law, and doctors in the three learned professions. Cambden reckons up four sorts of esquire. 1. The eldest sons of knights, and their eldest sons, in perpetual succession. 2. The younger sons of peers, and their eldest sons, in perpetual succession: which species Spelman calls *armigeri natalitii*. 3. Esquires created

* 5. Rich. II. stat. 2. chap. 4.—14. Rich. II. chap. 11.

by the king's letters patent, or other inveſtiture; and their eldeſt ſons. 4. Eſquires by virtue of their office; as juſtices of the peace, &c. To theſe may be added eſquires of knights of the bath, each of whom conſtitutes three at his inſtallation. All foreign, nay, Iriſh peers; and the eldeſt ſons of peers of Great Britain, who, though generally titular lords, are only eſquires in the law, and muſt be ſo named in all legal proceedings. As for *gentlemen*, ſays Sir Thomas Smith, whoever ſtudieth the laws of the realm, who ſtudieth in the univerſities, who profeſſeth liberal ſciences, who (to be ſhort) can live idly, and without manual labour, and will bear the port, charge, and countenance of a gentleman, he ſhall be called maſter, and taken for a gentleman. A *yeoman* is he that hath free land of forty ſhillings by the year; who is thereby qualified to ſerve on juries, vote for knights of the ſhire, and do any other act, which the law requires one that is *probus et legalis homo*. The reſt are *tradeſmen, artificers,* and *labourers.*

Of

OF THE

MILITARY

AND

MARITIME STATES.

THE military ſtate includes the whole of the ſoldiery; or, ſuch perſons as are peculiarly appointed for the defence and ſafeguard of the nation.

In the time of the Saxons it was in the hands of the dukes or heretochs, who were elected by the people in their full aſſembly.

Alfred firſt ſettled a national militia, of which we have no particulars; however, it left too much power in the dukes.

The

The feudal law, at the Norman conqueſt, brought 60,000 men into the field, from the number of knight's fees; which were to ſerve forty days in a year. This in time degenerated into pecuniary commutations, and was aboliſhed by ſtatute 12 Car. II. chap. 24. Beſides the knight's fees every man was obliged to provide arms according to his eſtate and degree, in order to keep the peace.

In Charles the ſecond's time, the power of the militia was aſcertained, and the order in which it now ſtands is principally built upon the ſtatutes then enacted.

The *maritime* ſtate is nearly related to the former. Firſt, for their ſupply. The power of impreſſing men for the ſea ſervice by the king's commiſſion, has been a matter of great diſpute, and ſubmitted to with reluctance; though it hath very clearly and learnedly been ſhewn, by Sir Michael Foſter, that the practice of impreſſing, and granting powers to the admiralty for that purpoſe, is of very ancient date, and hath been uniformly continued by a regular ſeries of precedents, to the preſent time: whence he concludes it a part of the common law. The difficulty
is

is from hence, that no statute hath expressly declared this power to be in the crown, though many of them very strongly imply it. The statute* speaks of mariners being arrested and retained for the king's service, as a thing well known, and practised without dispute, and provides a remedy against their running away. By a later statute†, if any waterman, who uses the river Thames, shall hide himself during the execution of any commission of pressing for the king's service, he is liable to heavy penalties. By another‡, no fisherman shall be taken by the queen's commission to serve as mariner; but the commission shall first be brought to two justices of the peace inhabiting near the sea coast, who are to chuse out and return such a number of able-bodied men, as in the commission are contained, to serve her majesty. And by others ||, especial protection ; are allowed to seamen in particular circumstances, to prevent them from being im-

* 2 Rich. II. chap. 24.
† 2 & 3 Ph. & M. chap. 16.
‡ 5 Eliz. chap. 5.
|| 7 & 8 Will. III. chap. 21.—2 Ann. chap. 6.— 4 & 5 Ann. chap. 19.—13 Geo. II. chap. 17.

pressed.

preffed. All which do moft evidently imply a power of impreffing to refide fomewhere, and, if any where, it muft from the fpirit of our conftitution, as well as from the frequent mention of the king's commiffion, refide in the crown alone.

Parifhes may bind out poor boys apprentices to mafters of merchantmen, who fhall be protected from any impreffing commiffion for three years. And if then impreffed, the mafter fhall be paid his wages*.

A failor cannot be arrefted for lefs than 20l. A foldier for lefs than 10l.

Upon the Norman conqueft all the lands were divided into what were called knight's fees, about 60,000; and for every fuch fee a knight or *miles*, was bound to attend the king forty days in every year. Statute of Weftminfter, 13 Edward I. chap. 6.—5 Henry IV.

To hang a man by martial law, is againft Magna Charta. chap. 29. And no foldier can be

---

* 2 Ann. chap. 6.
† 1 Geo. II. ftat. 2. chap. 14.

quartered

quartered on a subject by the petition of rights*.

Desertion in time of war is felony, and triable by a jury; and before the judges of the common law. 18 Henry VI. chap. 19. and 2 & 3 of Edward the Sixth.

* 31 Cha. II. chap. 1.

OF

MASTER AND SERVANT.

THE three great relations in private life are, 1. Master and servant. 2. Husband and wife. 3. Parent and child. In case of the death of parents, the law has provided a fourth relation, That of guardian and ward.

As to the several sorts of servants. Slavery cannot subsist in England.

I. The first sort of servants are *menial*, being *intra moenia*, or domestics; which according to contract may be for a longer or shorter term. All single men and women, having no visible livelihood, may be sent to services by two justices.

II. Another species are *apprentices*, usualy

ally bound for a term of years, to be maintained and inftructed by their mafters. Children of poor perfons may be apprenticed by the overfeers, with confent of two juftices, till twenty four-years of age. And it is held, that gentlemen of fortune and clergymen, are compellable to take them; but may be difcharged by two juftices.

III. A third fpecies are *labourers*.

IV. *Stewards, factors,* and *bailiffs*: which the law confiders as *pro tempore*.

A mafter may maintain an action at law for his fervant againft a ftranger; which he may not do for another man; or for beating or maiming his fervant. The mafter fhall be guilty of any trefpafs committed by his fervant, by his order, *nam qui facit per alium, facit per fe*. All thofe who ufually do bufinefs for another, whether relations or other, are deemed *quoad hoc* fervants; and payments made to them are good in law. A man is anfwerable for whatever his fervant may take up if he is ufually entrufted with fums of money; but not fo if he generally pays ready money himfelf to the tradefman for goods. In general the mafter is answerable for all negligences, annoyances and nusances occasioned by his servant, and this agrees with the civil law; *pater familias, ob alterius culpam tenetur, sive servi, sive liberi.*

OF

HUSBAND AND WIFE,

Or as the Old Law Books call them,

OF BARON AND FEME.

OUR law confiders marriages in no other light than as a civil contract. The *holinefs* of the matrimonial ftate is left intirely to the ecclefiaftical law. And, in this civil light, the law confiders it as valid, where the parties are willing to contract, and actually did contract in the proper terms required

Firft, they muft be *willing* to contract. *Confenfus, non concubitus, facit nuptias.*

Secondly, they muft be *able* to contract. Of this nature the difabilities are pre-contract; confanguinty; and affinity. But they

are

are esteemed valid to all civil purposes, unless separation is made during life of the parties. If any persons come together under these legal incapacities, it is a meretricious, and not a matrimonial union.

1. The first legal incapacity is a prior marriage, which is a felony, and the second marriage is void.

2. The second incapacity is want of age. But if at the age of consent they agree to continue together, it is a good marriage.

3. Another incapacity arises from want of consent of parents or guardians. By the common law and canon law, if the parties were of age of consent, there wanted no other concurrence; but, by several statutes, penalties of several kinds may be incurred.

4. A fourth incapacity is want of reason. The marriage of a lunatic, not being in a lucid interval, is void in law. It is held essential to a marriage, that the person performing the office be in orders; though this intervention of a priest is *juris positivi*, and not *juris naturalis aut divini*. Pope Innocent III. was the first who ordained the celebration to be in a church; before it was a civil contract.

Marriages

Marriages are diffolved by death, or divorce which is of two kinds, one total, the other partial; *a menfa et thoro*, from bed and board. Adultery formerly only incurred the latter; though of late years it divorces *a vinculo matrimonii*, but allows *alimony* to the wife.

The hufband and wife are one perfon in law: the wife is *faemina viro co-operta*, or is faid to be *covert-baron*. All contracts between them are void. She may be attorney for her hufband; for that implies a reprefentation of her lord. If the wife be indebted before marriage the hufband is to pay the debt. She can bring no action in her own name, unlefs her hufband has abjured the realm, or is banifhed: for then he is dead in law. In the civil law they are confidered as two diftinct perfons; and a woman may fue and be fued, without her hufband. In execution of deeds, fhe muft be folely and fecretly examined, to learn if her act be voluntary. The difabilities which the wife lies under, are for the moft part intended for her protection and benefit. So great a favourite is the female fex of the laws of England.

OF

PARENT

AND

CHILD.

THE next, and moſt univerſal relation in nature is, between parent and child.

Children are of two ſorts; legitimate and ſpurious. Legitimate is he that is born in lawful wedlock. *Pater eſt quem nuptiae demonſtrant.*

The duties of parents bind them, as to maintenance, protection, and education. If a parent runs away, the pariſh officers ſhall ſeize his rents, goods, and chattels, for thoſe

those purposes. No person is bound to provide a maintenance for his issue, where they are able to provide for themselves. A parent may maintain and uphold his children in law-suits, and quarrels. The last duty is, in giving them an *education* suitable to their station in life. It is in general left to the discretion of those in good circumstances; yet a man incurs a penalty, who shall send his son to any seminary abroad for the purpose of being instructed in the romish religion.

The consent of the parent is absolutely necessary, to confirm a marriage, if the child is under-age.

An illegitimate child or bastard, is one that is not only begotten, but born, out of matrimony; and in the case of a divorce, all issue are bastards.

If a man is charged by a woman with-child, who is unmarried, if she swears it, he must give security for its maintenance, or appear at the next quarter sessions to dispute and try the fact. A bastard cannot be heir to any one, for being *filius nullius*, he is of kin to nobody; and was formerly incapable

pable of holding any dignity in the church. By the tranfcendent power of an act of parliament, as in the cafe of John of Gaunt's baftard children, he may be made legitimate.

OF

GUARDIAN

AND

WARD.

THE reciprocal duties are the fame, *pro tempore*, as between the father and child. The guardian, when the ward comes of age, is bound to give an account of all he has tranfacted on his account, and muſt anſwer for all loſſes by wilful neglect or default. In large concerns it is uſual to indemnify themſelves by acting under, and accounting before the officers of the court of chancery. For the chancelor is the ſupreme guardian of all infants, lunatics and idiots.

A male at twelve years of age may take the oath

oath of allegiance; at fourteen is at years of difcretion, may confent to marriage, choofe his guardian; and if his difcretion be actually proved, may make a teftament of his worldy eftate; at feventeen he may be an executor; and at twenty-one may aliene his lands, goods, and chattels.

A female at feven years of age may be betrothed; at nine is entitled to dower; at twelve is at years of maturity, and may confent or difagree to marriage; at fourteen is at years of difcretion; at feventeen may be an executrix; and at twenty-one may difpofe of herfelf and lands. The full age of both is twenty-one years, which age is completed the day before the anniverfary of a perfon's birth; who till that time is ftiled in law, an infant.

An infant can aliene his lands under the direction of the court of chancery, or other courts of equity. An infant who has an advowfon, may prefent to the benefice when it becomes void,

OF

CORPORATIONS.

THE firſt diviſion of Corporations is into *aggregate* and *ſole*. The firſt conſiſts of many perſons united together into one ſociety, and kept up by a ſucceſſion of members: of which kind are the mayor and commonalty of a city, the head and fellows of a college, the dean and chapter of a cathedral church.

Corporations ſole conſiſt of one only and his ſucceſſors, who are incorporated by law, to give ſome legal capacities, which they could not otherwiſe have individually. The king is a ſole corporation: ſo is a biſhop: and ſome deans: and every parſon and vicar.

Another

Another divifion of corporations, fole or aggregate, is into *ecclefiaftical* and *lay*. All for the fame purpofe, of perpetuating a fucceffion of perfons neceffary for the carrying on certain things, which may have the fame effect, without end.—For the prefent perfon and him, or thofe who lived feven centuries ago, are in law one and the fame.

I. The king's confent is neceffary to the erection of any corporation, exprefsly or impliedly, by an act of the king, or prefcription. A corporation muft have a name and by that name fue, and be fued, and do all legal acts.

II. A corporation has fome things neceffarily belonging to it. 1. To have perpetual fucceffion.. 2. To fue or be fued, implead or to be impleaded, grant or receive, by it's corporate name. 3. To purchafe lands, and hold them, for the benefit of their fucceffors. 4. To have a common feal; which binds and unites the feveral affents of the individuals. 5. To make bye-laws or private ftatutes; which are binding upon themfelves, unlefs contrary to law.

A corporation muft always appear by its attorney;

attorney; being in it's nature invisible. It cannot commit crimes or misdemeanors, nor suffer such injuries which belong to individuals; nor can it receive punishment, nor is liable to attainder, forfeiture, &c.

The general *duties* of bodies politic, are, the acting up to the end or design, for which they were created by their founder.

III. Corporations being composed of human creatures are subject to frailties, therefore the law has appointed proper persons to visit, inquire into, and correct irregularities. In ecclesiastical corporations, the ordinary is their visitor; in lay, the founder, his heirs, or assigns are the visitors. In general the king is the sole founder of all civil corporations, and the right of visitation results to him.

Colleges are deemed lay-corporations.

IV. Corporations may be dissolved in several ways; which dissolution is it's civil death. 1. By act of parliament. 2. By the natural death of all it's members. 3. By surrender of it's franchises into the hands of the king, which is a kind of suicide. 4. By forfeiture through negligence or abuse of it's
franchises.

franchifes; and the regular courfe is by a writ of *quo warranto*, to inquire by what warrant, the members hold or exercife their right and power, having forfeited it, by fuch and fuch proceedings.

LAW

OF

DESCENTS.

1. INHERITANCES shall lineally descend to the issue of the person last actually seised, in *infinitum*, but shall never lineally ascend.

2. The male issue shall be admitted before the female.

3. Where there are two or more males in degree, the eldest only shall inherit; but the females all together.

4. The lineal descents in *infinitum* of any person deceased shall represent their ancestor; that is shall stand in the same place, as the person

perſon himſelf would have done, had he been living.

5. On failure of lineal deſcendants or iſſue, of the perſon laſt ſeiſed, the inheritance ſhall deſcend to the blood of the firſt purchaſer; ſubject to the three preceding rules.

6. The collateral kinſman of the whole blood.

7. In collateral inheritances the male ſtocks ſhall be preferred to the female; that is, kindred derived from the blood of the male anceſtors ſhall be admitted before thoſe from the blood of the female, unleſs where the lands have in fact deſcended from a female.

This abſtract may ſerve as a manual or remembrancer. But for thoſe who deſire to have a full knowledge of the intentions and origins of the law; an application to the book itſelf is abſolutely neceſſary.

OF

SOME

VICISSITUDES

OF OUR

GLOBE.

TRANSLATED

FROM THE

FRENCH OF MONS. DE PAUW.

OF

S O M E

VICISSITUDES OF OUR GLOBE.

TRANSLATED

FROM THE

FRENCH OF MONS. DE PAUW.

AS in this year, 1764, one may already reckon forty-nine different fyftems, propofed for explaining the difafters and phyfical revolutions which our fingular planet has undergone; it appeared to me lefs difficult to hazard a new one amongft them, than to difcufs fo many different opinions.

I undertake therefore, fir, to communicate to you fome obfervations which I have made at different times, and which in their prefent ftate cannot be confidered as more than the foundation of an hypothefis.

It

It is very surprising that the three great capes or promontories of the Earth, viz. Cape Horn, the Cape of Good Hope, and that of Diemen's land (New Guinea) should be turned to the south. It is proper to consider this remarkable position in the small map of Mr. Bellin, where it is more perceptible than in the common maps of the world.

The points of the three great continents directed towards the south, makes me suspect that immense volumes of water have rolled with violence from the south to the north, by different directions; and that they have made breaches wherever the soft and sandy soils have given way to the impulse of the ocean.* The capes, the most famous after those which I have named, are situated in the same sense, being more or less oblique to the south pole: such as Cape Comorin in

---

* One may say that the three great promontories of the Mediterranean are are also turned towards the south; the point of Calabria, the Morea, and the Crimea. Whatsoever they may be more or less diverging from the points of south-east and south-west is of no importance, since it is true, that a line drawn from these three promontories would cut the equator.

Asia,

Afia, that of Malacca in the peninfula of that name, St. Mary in Madagafcar, Oftokoi-nos in the peninfula of Kamfcatfka, Sandeck in Nova Zembla, Arria in the great ifland of Jefo Gazima, Farewell in Greenland, St. Lucar in California, and that of Bahama in Florida; when one fees all thefe objects in the great, it is unneceffary to regard thofe little points minutely, which advance more or lefs into the fea; which are indiftinctly called capes or promontories, becaufe the language of Geography is like many other fciences, very poor in words. From whence it happens that the ideas are confounded for want of efficacious and proper terms, neverthelefs there is a very effential difference between a cape which bounds a vaft continent, or great ifland, and a cape which is only a faliant angle, formed by particular accidents, attending the finuofity of the coaft.

The greateft breach the waters have made in our continent, appears between Africa and New Holland to Cape Comorin; which being formed of vaft impenetrable rocks, it apparently divided the currents from the fouth.

south. One of these torrents beat out of it's first course, seems to have absorbed all the space occupied at this day by the Red Sea; of which the Adriatic Gulph is in my opinion a continuation. For I imagine that the same force which carried the waters into the land at the Babel-Mandel, made them continue to the neighbourhood of Venice, in surmounting the Istmus of Suez; which is since dried up, either by the retreat of the Mediterranean, or by the dimunition of the Red Sea. In examining the nature of the soil on the Istmus of Suez one may easily perceive that it has been formerly covered by the sea, and Necho or Nechao, who governed Egypt more than two and twenty hundred years ago, undertook to cut through this tongue of land which incommoded him.

As to the Persian Gulph, it seems to have been produced by the same irruption and tendency of the ocean to the north pole. The ancients were very reasonable in supposing that the Caspian Sea was a prolonggation of the Persian Gulph, which has never been more probable than since it's exact figure is known from the charts which vice-admiral Kruys has inserted in his great

atlas

atlas of the courfe of the Volga. In running over the intermediate fpace from the Gulph of Perfia to the Cafpian Sea on an ideal line traced between the 71ft and 72d degree of longitude, from the Cape to that of Ferrabat, one falls upon indubitable veftiges of the fea's ancient bed : a wide champain country of moving fands, mixed with fragments of fhells and remains of marine fubftances. In going beyond thefe dry plains an entrance is made into the great defart of fand, which is 40 parafangues to the north of Ifpahan. In the depth of this folitude, enormous mountains of falt are frequently fpread upon the furface for many leagues every way. This canton is at this day called the Salt Sea by the inhabitants, although fituated very much in the continent, and our maps name it, Mare Salfum. On the right of this region of falt runs a line fandy hills which the winds have heaped together, and which are prolonged to the fouth eaft, even to the foot of Mount Albours, which has formerly been a large volcano, that has been extinguifhed by the retreat of the fea. In advancing conftantly under the fame meridian beyond Coucheften the Earth inclines, and continues floping perceptibly to Ferrabat.

This

This line which I have defcribed as an ancient trace or antique bafon of the ocean, penetrates the heart of Perfia, which is indeed a dry and fterile region, where water is deficient to fuch a degree, that without the help of artificial canals, and the invention of aqueducts, it would be difficult to fubfift; as we find in reading Chardin and Tavernier.

We know that in many countries very diftant from each other, that in digging, whole forefts are found under the earth from twenty to fixty feet. If thefe forefts had been felled by the great revolutions of the Globe, they ought, according to my fyftem, to prefent themfelves as foffil trees, of which the roots were turned to the fouth, and the branches to the north. But from what I have feen, and from the report of others who have examined the pofition of thefe trees, buried in the bogs and marfhes of Frizeland, Holland, and Groningen, it is certain that they were found with the foot lying towards the north-eaft, and the crown to the oppofite point: which proves that the force which proftrated them, was directed from the north-eaft to the fouth-weft.

But why fhould we attribute that to the general

general viciffitudes of our planet, which may have been produced by particular accidents? It was the inundation of the Cimbric Cherfonefus (Denmark), which according to the calculation of Picard, happened about 340 years before Chrift, which buried the forefts of Frizeland, and formed all thofe drowned marfhes which reach from Schelling to Bentheim. The foffil trees difcovered in England, in the county of Lancafter, have alfo long paffed for monuments of the fame kind; but upon examination of fome naturalifts, it has been found that the roots of thofe trees had been cut with an hatchet; which, together with the medals of Julius Cefar, that are found there at the depth of eighteen feet, fuffice to determine pretty nearly the date of their fall; fince it is very probable that it was the work of the Romans to drive out the favage Britons hidden there, after their defeat in the plains: and all Europe, if we except Italy alone, was one immenfe foreft eighteen hundred years ago.

I have obferved, with aftonifhment, that there is fo much more dry land on this fide the equator than beyond it, where there is more fea.

The continent of land at the south pole cannot have the extent generally assigned to it, for the navigators who have been acquainted with the south sea to the 55th degree of latitude on our hemisphere, and to the 60th on that opposite to ours, have not fallen in with any coast or discovered any indication of such great continent.* In short, let one calculate however one may, we are constrained to allow a much larger portion of continent to be situated in the northern latitude than on the southern, from whence the waters have made their incisions.

It is very *mal à propos* that it has been sustained by some philosophers, that this unequal partition could not exist, under pretence that the Globe would lose its equilibrium, for want of a sufficient counterpoize at the south pole. It is true that a cubic foot of salt water does not weigh equal to a cubic foot of earth; but it ought to be recollected, that under the ocean there may be strata of matters, of which the specific weight may vary infinitely, and that the small depth of a sea spread over a great surface,

* This was written before the voyages of Cooke, Phipps, and others.

may counterbalance the places, where there is lefs fea, but where it is deeper.

I obferve with equal furprize, that almoft all that part of the Globe placed directly under the equinoctial line, is at this day covered by the ocean; which is very difficult to combine with what has been generally faid of the circular elevation the earth ought to have at the equator. If this elevation was fuch as has been fuppofed, it is manifeft that the waters tending to an equilibrium, would go to accumulate themfelves to the heighth of five leagues under the poles fo that there would remain a large zone of dry land between the tropics. But one fees by the maps, that the contrary is the fact; it muft be agreed then, that the hydroftatic laws are falfe and illufory, or that it is impoffible, that the length of the terreftrial axis fhould be to that of the terreftrial equator, as 174 to 175. Mr. Buffon is not the only one who has accufed this meafure of a want of exactnefs,* other naturalifts and aftronomers

* Mr. Buffon pretends that the length of the terreftrial equator is to that of the axis, as 230 to 229. Although this calculation feems to approach much nearer to the truth, and lefs to contradict the phenomena, it can

mers have equally perceived the inconvenience refulting from this evident error of cofmography.

It is demonftrated that a much greater degree of cold is felt in advancing towards the fouth pole than towards the north; whilft the fun's courfe is within a fecond as many degrees in one latitude as the other, and fends an equal quantity of rays to our antipodes as to us. Neverthelefs, there is a great difference in the heat, in the like feafons, in correfpondent heights, under the fame meridian. I have often reflected on this phenomenon, and no explication has been prefented to my mind more fatisfactory than what has been mentioned. I would fay, that I attribute this difference of temperature to the greater quantity of habitable land in our latitude, than beyond the equator. That which produces the effect to aftonifh us, is, that the furface of water cools the atmofphere infinitely more than the fame furface of continent: it is perceptible even on great lakes

---

can only be admitted as a guefs. It is fufficient to know that the Globe is not fo flat at the poles as has been reprefented, and perhaps we may never arrive at the true length of the axis, and of that of the terreftrial equator.

and

and rivers, without the affiftance of the thermometer.

The augmentation of cold towards the fouth pole, adds a new degree of probability to my opinion concerning the fmall extent of land near that pole. If there were fuch a depth and circumference as fufpected, fo much cold could not be felt in going to the fouth. In the northern latitude the ices are generally melted, at moft, by the beginning of May. Veffels get to the 79th and even to the 80th degree; but the navigators who were defirous to advance fouthward, have always met with fogs and ice iflands, whether in fummer or winter, under the fixtieth* parallel : fo that we have been 500 leagues, or twenty degrees, farther to the north than to the fouth; which without doubt is very furprifing. In vain would Mr. Buffon perfuade us, that the ices in the South Seas are formed by the great rivers which defcend from the Auftral lands: that does not refolve the difficulty, fince the queftion is not how the ices are formed, but it remains to be proved why they fhould diffolve in fummer in the 80th

* Capt. Phipps went to 81 N. and Capt. Cooke to 61¼ S. fince this Letter of Mr. De P.

degree in our latitude, and are never melted, in any feafon, in the 60th degree of oppofite latitude. Let us agree then, that the occafion of the cold being fo conftantly rigorous there, is, that the immenfe furface of the ocean prevents the atmofphere from being fufficiently heated, to diffolve the mountains of ice which float under the fame parallel where all the Argonauts have been ftopt. The Prefident de Broffes, in his Hiftory of the Navigators to the Auftral Continents, pretends, that this phenomenon is caufed by the variation of the ecliptic; but I avow fincerely that I comprehend nothing of this explication; befides, as it is not proved that the ecliptic is fubject to any fuch variation, it appears to me that the Prefident fhould have begun with a demonftration of the caufe, before he deduced the effect.

If a force from the fouth has pufhed the waters to the north, another power of re-action fhould then, and at this time, continue to bring them back towards the point from which they departed. The obfervations of the Swedifh naturalifts leave us no room to doubt of the retreat of the fea from the north; which has lowered a little more than

than four feet fix inches in a century. It is very true that the clergy of Sweden, apparently hurt at this difcovery, prefented a memorial, in 1747, to the ftates of the kingdom, in which it accufed all the learned of herefy, who fpoke or wrote in favour of this diminution of the fea; becaufe this fyftem, as they faid, tended to weaken the blind faith we owe to the antient jewifh books. The celebrated Mr. Olof Dalin oppofed facts, experiments and demonftrations, to thefe fcandalous imputations of the clergy ; to whom the ftates impofed filence, under pain of chaftifement: but a bifhop of Finland, Mafter John Brouaillius or Brouillonius, dared, in defiance of this wife command of the general diet, to publifh a differtation, in which he endeavours to prove, that the fifteen philofophers who had obferved this retreat of the ocean, were fo many blind men, becaufe they had no bifhopricks. I have read the whole of this differtation of Mafter Brouaillius, who banifhed in his little diocefe of Abo, does not appear to have been inftructed in the ftate of the queftion in agitation at Upfal and Stockholm: he amufes himfelf in proving that no drop of water could poffibly be be annihilated; and if that is a fact fays he, why will thefe damnable Sectaries of Mr. Maillet infift, that the northern fea is lower at this time, than in that of Tycho Brahe? but Meffieurs Dalin and Swedenburgh have never advanced that a drop of water could be annihilated, they have only concluded, that the fea in retiring from the north, carried itfelf to the fouth.

I am profoundly ignorant of the caufe of the firft progreffion of the ocean towards the Boreal circle, as of the contrary one, which gives it the retrogade march to the oppofite point ; but if there is any juftice in my obfervations, we ought to conclude, that there exifts a periodical motion in nature as yet unknown, which occafions an alternate flux of water from one pole to the other; fo that deluges are not uncertain events, but neceffary effects of the conftruction of our globe : and it was the fentiment of the ancient Egyptian philofophers, who were, doubtlefs, the depofitaries of a great number of memoirs and hiftorical monuments concerning the deftinies of our planet. Thefe philofophers told Solon, *Certis temporum curriculis illuvies immiffa cælitus omnia populatur, multaque et varia hominum*

hominum fuere exitia, ideo qui fuccedunt, et literis et mufis orbati funt.* From whence we may infer, that they confidered deluges as periodical events, and the ages of ignorance and ruin of the arts, as neceffary confequences of them.

If the experiments made on the coaft of Denmark and Sweden, demonftrate to us, that at this day the waters return from the north to the fouth, we are no longer aftonifhed to find more dry land on our fide the equator, than on that beyond us. If the diminution of the fea is perceptible in the boreal regions, as they affure us, fome one will fay, that we ought to perceive fomething of the like in our little Mediterranean: although this confequence is not to be efteemed exactly juft, yet authorities are not wanting to prove that, in effect, the Mediterranean does lower from age to age; and I cannot guefs why Manfredi attacked this hypothefis. He agreed, that in comparing the modern meafurements with thofe of the ancients, that the bottom of the Mediterranean was much higher; from whence he concludes, that the level ought to follow the fame proportion, and to rife equally with the increafe of the

* Plato in Timeo.

bottom. This is a sophism, or a captious reasoning; for the Mediterranean cannot rise above its ancient bounds, by the increase of its bottom: for in proportion to the elevation of that, an equal volume of water would be carried off through the straights of Gibraltar; otherwise the coasts, which formerly laid dry, would be drowned by becoming lower than the superficies of the sea. But in Italy we see an infinity of places which the sea has abandoned, as well as the port of Ravenna; and it is impossible to find one place where it has intruded itself upon the coast: which must infallibly have happened if Manfredi had reasoned justly. It must not be objected to what I say, that the Pontine marshes have never abounded in water so much as in our days; for these marshes are not formed, as some believe, by the inundations of the Mediterranean, but by the torrents and rains which descend from the Appenines, which settle themselves more or less in those low lands for want of canals, or issues, to run off.

It is absurd to imagine, as Manfredi has done, that the bottom of the bason of the Mediterranean has been raised by the sand and

and mud introduced by the currents of the rivers; for by this reafoning, all Egypt ought to have been excavated by the Nile, Italy by the Po, and Germany by the Danube; whereas the beds of thofe rivers have not vifibly been hollowed within a thoufand years paft.

The fediment which running waters bear away with them, is not fo confiderable as it appears; there being a real optical illufion in it. The waters of any river, however thick and muddy to the appearance of the fight, does not contain quite fixty grains of earth, in one hundred and twenty pounds of water. In fettling fome water of the Nile in a glafs tube, the fediment was found to have only the eight of a line* in a volume of water, which feemed to have fifty times more mud than was obtained by precipitation.

Of courfe it muft happen that earthquakes muft fometimes ravage our Globe, but I doubt if they have ever been fo deftructive as inundations. I am aftonifhed that no hiftory or tradition, fhould ever

* A line is the 12th part of an inch.

have

have taken notice of any memorable cataſtrophe, occaſioned by earthquakes, between the 52d and 61ſt degrees of north latitude, in the heart of the continent. I do not believe that any town in Germany has ever been overturned as Liſbon was, nor has there been any ſuch example in the north of France: it is only when we advance towards the pole, or the line beyond thoſe points mentioned, that earthquakes become both frequent and terrible.

Another obſervation, no leſs intereſting, is, that the greater part of the volcanos on our hemiſphere, are ſituated on iſlands, or very near to the ſea: Hecla in Iceland, Etna in Sicily, and Veſuvius on the Mediterranean coaſt. One may reckon of ſmall volcanos, the Lipary iſlands, which often ſmoke without their having any communication with Veſuvius or Etna, as ſome have ſuſpected. Amongſt the great volcanos may be reckoned, the Paranucan in the iſland of Java, Conapy in the iſle of Banda, and Balaluan in Sumatra: the iſland of Ternate has a burning mountain equal to Etna. There are alſo volcanos in the iſlands of Ferando, Chiangen, and Ximo; in ſhort, amongſt all the iſlands, iflands, great and fmall, which compofe the empire of Japan, as well as the Manilla iflands; they have all one, more or lefs confiderable: the fame in the Azores, the Cape Verd iflands, and above all that of Del Fuego. In the Canary iflands is the Pic of Teneriffe, which yet fends out rolling maffes of fmoke; the fires of which has raifed that immenfe pyramid of irregularly piled pieces of calcined rock, covered with cinders and lava. The iflands of the Papous, St. Helena, Socra, Milo, and Mayn, have alfo their furnaces more or lefs illuminated.

It is impoffible to indicate upon the whole furface of the continent, a twentieth part of the number of volcanos that I can name upon the iflands; and that fince the greater part of the burning mountains are extinct, which are faid to have exifted in Afia, as well as thofe, the ruins of which are to be feen on the coafts of Angola and Congo.

This fingular pofition of volcanos in the iflands makes me fufpect that fea water is a neceffary ingredient to produce the inflammation of fulphureous and ferruginous pyrites, which feem to be the principal aliment of all the known volcanos. It is certain, from experiments

periments made on these species of pyrites, that they never burn but from being in contact with water, or a moist atmosphere; which may be attributed to the property which iron has to decompose sulphur by the means of water. By the lavas discovered in the Pyrenees, in the Alps, and the mountains of Auvergne, and Provence, and in many vallies of the Appenines, it is concluded, that all these places have anciently been volcanos, the lavas being of those substances, whose origin must have proceeded from burning mountains.

But why are the furnaces, placed at this day on the terra firma, extinct, whilst those on the islands continue to burn? The cause, in my opinion, is very clear; which is, that the sea having retreated from their neighbourhood, the fire has ceased because the decomposition of the pyrites can no longer take place in the bowels of the earth, for want of a sufficient quantity of water. We may see by Tournefort's Description of Mount Ararat, that there are many mouths from whence cataracts of fire have formerly been vomited, which has persuaded me, that the sea has formerly washed the foot of that mountain, which in our days is at a

great

great diftance from the coaft; for which reafon it neither throws out fire nor fmoke.

To attribute the extinction of volcanos on the firm land, to the total want of philogiftic matter, is, to propofe a manifeft error; fince there is no reafon to maintain that thefe fubftances fhould have been confumed there, rather then on the iflands, or fea coafts. Vefuvius has burned more than three thoufand years; which I fhall endeavour to demonftrate by fome arguments, which may perhaps be fatisfactory to you.

In pufhing on the diggings of Herculaneum as far as have been practicable, they have at length come to the pavements of the ftreets and foundations of the houfes of that buried city. After taking up many of the ftones which made a part of the pavements and foundations, and examining to what clafs of Lythology they belonged, it is found, by the effays made, that they were of Lava cut into fquares: fo that we have found vitrified fubftances from the furnace of fome volcano, in the time that the Aufonians, or Arrunci, built Herculaneum; which is one of the moft ancient cities of Italy, fince it fell under the

power

power of the firft colonies of the Greeks, or Phenicians, that penetrated Europe by the Mediterranean. It is impoffible to fix the foundation later than 1330 years before Chrift; fo that three thoufand and ninety-eight years have paffed away, from that event to our days; and as Vefuvius continues to furnifh the fame fort of lavas, it is a proof that it burned long before the foundation of Herculaneum, where thefe fcoria were employed to ftrengthen the principal edifices. Etna, at this time fo famous for its burnings, had burnt for many ages before the birth of Homer and Hefiod. If the combuftible matter of thefe two great furnaces of the globe have not been drained, during fuch a prodigious lapfe of ages, we have no authority to fuppofe that the volcanos of our continent have been extinguifhed from any other caufe than the want of nourifhment.

Vefuvius might contain in its folid convexity, from its bafe to its funnel, 1510,460,879 cubic feet of earth, and other fubftances; neverthelefs, if we calculate what it has thrown out of cinders, fand, lava, pumice ftones, pyrites, phofphoric ftones, pozzolane,

zolane,* scoria, iron drofs, bitumen, sal-ammoniac, allum, sulphur, and metals in fusion, we shall see that the mass and volume are more considerable than the whole body of the mountain; of which was ejected from it's funnel, in 1737, an amazing torrent of liquified matters, calculated by Francesco Serrao at 319,658,161 cubic feet: it could not take a less quantity in the like flood, which submerged Herculaneum and Pompeia. During the celebrated burning of Etna, in 1683, there departed from it two rivers of lava, each of thirty palms† in depth, and which overflowed eleven leagues round: *Quifque fuum populatus iter.* From which we may easily conjecture, what ought to be the capacity of the reservoir, or rather abyss, from whence these calcined and vitrified matters were extracted by the combined force of fire and water.

Whatever has been written hitherto, relative to the formation of mountains, is subject to so many difficulties, that it is impossible, however desirous one may be, to be satisfied

* Land resembling that of Pozzuoli in Italy.

† The Roman Palm is twelve fingers, or three quarters of a foot.

with the fyftems propofed on this fubject; which have abfolutely loft all credit, fince it is known, that the moft high mountainous points, are in no part of the world covered with marine remains, fuch as fhells, dendrites,* or other petrifications, under whatever name they may be known: the fea then has never furmounted thofe heights, which fo many naturalifts have advanced, to give a confiftence to the vague ideas on which they have founded their hypothefis. I can never be perfuaded that it is by the fea that thofe rocks have been formed, whofe beds, of the fame fort of ftone, we often fee prolonged for a fpace of three leagues. How fhould the waters affemble fo many fubftances of a fimilar kind, and place them in another place; at the fame time preventing all mixtures of heterogeneous matter; in the moment of cohefion of thefe lapidific particles? It is in no wife aftonifhing that fragments of fhells are found in marbles, becaufe marbles are only co-agulations; but it has never been feen, nor ever will, that any fhells are found in rock ftone: which proves to a certainty, that this fort of ftone, of which whole mountains are to be found, has never

* Petrified corals.

been

been decompofed or recompofed by the waves of the fea, that it is an homogenous fubftance, primitive, and of the age of the world. I fhould be as well pleafed that any body would write a Treatife on the Formation of the Stars, as that of thefe rocks, which have been raifed by the puiffant hands of creative nature, to which we are indebted for our fmall planet, where philofophers reafon. It appears, that in their reafoning upon mountains, that they have neglected to make a very neceffary diftinction, for they have confounded the great convex elevations with what they generally term mountains ; fuch as that of Oriental Tartary, which may be regarded as the moft enormous protuberance upon the furface of the globe. To be affured of the certainty of this elevation, we have only to obferve the confiderable and vaft rivers that defcend from this declivity, in all it's different directions ; which fhews alfo, that this land is very high and convex, without our being able to find any fingle mountain comparable with thofe of Switzerland.

The principal rivers, which from this heighth fhape their courfes towards the cardinal points, are, the Oby, which is dif-

charged

charged to the north into the gulph of Obfkaia; Guba, the Genifka or Geniffea, which is loft in the frozen ocean, oppofite to the point of Nova Zembla; the Chatanga, the Lena, the Jana, and the Kowinna, all four of which fall into the fame ocean; the Uda, and L'Amour or Sagalicin Ulla, which carry their waters towards the north-eaft, into the fea of Kamfkatfca; the Hoang,* or Saffron River, which rifing at Kokonor, in the country of the Eleuths, pierces the great wall of China, and after a courfe of eighteen hundred Chinefe lis, enters, by the eaft, into the gulph of Nankin. I might reckon yet the Ganges and the Indus, which run directly fouthward; but as they do not defcend from Tartary, properly fo called, I do not enumerate them; but I place here the Jalk and the Jemba, which winding to the weft, difcharge themfelves into the Cafpian. There are not any of thefe rivers, all larger than the Seine, which have not their rife in Tartary; nor any of them that defcend from this convexity, of which I have been fpeaking, which are not more confiderable than the Jefuits fay, who pretend to have meafured them: but this enterprize would exact more Geo-

metrical

* Called in our maps Kiang.

metrical knowledge, in taking levels, than
such men as Gerbillon and Verbist possessed.

Switzerland is, in miniature, with regard
to Europe, that which Tartary is for Asia,
in the great; with this exception, that Switzerland has perpendicular mountains infinitely more elevated than that of Sabatzi-Nos; in the part of Tartary called Jakutian
Siberia by the moderns. If the diminution
of steep mountains is as effective as they
are willing to persuade us, Switzerland,
from being pyramidal, will become a convex
elevation at the expiration of many millions
of ages.

The rains, melted snows, the springs,
and torrents, which descend from the mountainous point, ought to detach and draw
with them into the vallies, by the simple
effort of their weight and fall, a certain
quantity of earth, stones and sand. The angles
and sides most exposed to the action and shock
of the air, should be cracked and decomposed;
the winds should sweep away with them the
small particles; the pillars which support
those vast masses of rock, which stand singly, should in the end sink under their load,
and occasion such frightful overwhelmings
as

as that which crufhed the town of Pleurs. All this is true, but the time required to decay the fummit of a mountain and to flatten it, may alfo wear out our planet, and in the end, bring nature into the laft ftage of decrepitude. It fuffices for us to begin to be, for us to fee ourfelves condemned to a termination. Our exiftence will laft no more than five hundred years, if we believe Newton; who has calculated that the largeft of the thirty-nine comets known at this time, will ftrike fo violently againft the fun in the year 2255, that there will be no hope, after that accident, of his being able to illumine the inhabitants of this world. There muft be a great pleafure in predicting misfortunes, fince the wifeft of philofophers could not refift the inclination to prophecy, and to announce the inftant of the combuftion of the univerfe; a tafte for which, he moft likely acquired in commentating the Revelations: fo far is it dangerous to read books one does not comprehend, and more fo yet, to write commentaries on them.

As it is upon the greateft convex elevations of our continent that we ought to look for the moft ancient people, there is no doubt but that, in this refpect, the Tartars

carry

carry it before all others: so the Greeks and Romans, however intoxicated with their own antiquity, without any scruple, admitted the Scythians to be the eldest of mankind. The passage, the most interesting in my opinion, of the abbreviator Justin, is, the first chapter of the second book, where he gives an account of a contest between some Egyptians and Scythians, concerning the antiquity of their nations. The Scythian said to the inhabitants of Egypt, *Scythiam adeo editiorem omnibus terris esse, ut cuncta flumina ibi nata in mæotim, tum deinde in ponticum et Ægyptium mare decurrant; his argumentis superatis Ægyptis antiquiores semper Scythæ visi.*

There is nothing more surprizing, than to see some geographical assertions respecting Tartary, verified in our days; which were set forth by Trogeius Pompeius, who lived under Augustus, which he had found in some histories much earlier than the age of Augustus. The Chinese own that they descend from the Tartars, who descend from none; and who, by consequence, merit the title of Aborigines, which so many nations have so often usurped.

I have already observed, in my Philosophical

phical Researches upon the Americans, that mountains, of whatever heighth they might be, could not serve as a safe retreat to the inhabitants of a country destroyed by inundations; because, such mountains being more dry and sterile in proportion to their altitude, could not provide the alimentary plants necessary for the sustenance of families and herds of cattle: ten persons could not live ten days upon the summit of Mount Jura,§ assailed at once with cold and hunger. It is upon such convexities as that of Tartary, where the remains of the human race might hope to find asylum against the crush of elements and the fury of inundation.

If the Tartars had not, during their wars, so frequently destroyed the libraries formed by the learned of Thibet; if a worthless emperor of China had not ordered his subjects, on pain of death, to burn all the books* and manuscripts

§ In Switzerland.

* The general destruction of Chinese books, by a Barbarian whose name ought not to be pronounced; the burning of the library of Alexandria, under Julius Cesar; the burning of a second, in part, re-established in the same place under the Caliph Omar; and the destruction of the ancient Greek authors, under Pope Gregory; are, in my

manuscripts they could gather together in upper Asia, we might, without doubt, have discovered in them many facts that would have thrown light on the history of our globe; which appears so modern when we consult the monuments of men, and so ancient when we appeal to nature. A naturalist, whose ideas and destiny were equally whimsical, flattered himself, some years ago, that he had discovered the means of finding the age of petrifications; from whence a theory might be deduced to come at the age of the world: but it is a delusion, to be persuaded that a method, in itself defective, can ever lead to a result that is exact and just.

The late emperor having asked permission of the grand seignior, to take up some of the

---

my opinion, the most sorrowful events in the history of the human kind; because they have deprived us of an infinity of knowledge, which is not in the power of man to recover. The archives of the world were lost: nevertheless, our chronologists boldly fix the epoch of the origin of all nations. To observe the arrogance with which they offer their vain calculations, one would imagine they had read over and over all the books, and all the manuscripts, destroyed in China, Thibet, Egypt, and Rome; the titles even of which, they are ignorant.

Vol. I.   F f f   piles

piles on which Trajan had founded the bridge he threw over the Danube in Servia, on a cloſe examination they found, that the petrification had advanced about three quarters of an inch, in ſomething more than fifteen hundred years: from whence it was concluded, that a piece of wood of equal thickneſs, and of the heighth of forty feet, would petrify an inch in twenty centuries, and take up nine hundred thouſand years to arrive at a complete tranſmutation: but as the trunks of petrified trees have been dug up, whoſe length have been forty feet, let one judge by this mode, of the time that they muſt have been cut down and buried. This reaſoning would be admirable if it did not contain a defect, which weakens it to a degree, as to make it of no value: the paralogiſm conſiſts in the ſuppoſition that there are no waters, earths, or ſubſtances of petrification, where it is carried on in a ſhorter time than in this part of the Danube where Trajan's bridge was ſituated: there are, doubtleſs, many places where the lapidific juices are more abundant, and where the animal and vegetable ſubſtances are ſooner tranſmuted by the impregnation of theſe juices. As it is impoſſible to determine the
mean

mean duration of time that any body, whatever, may require to be petrified, becaufe of the infinite variety of circumſtances, earths, waters and air, and even of the poſitions of the bodies; it may eaſily be conceived that this method, incapable of being perfected, or even meliorated, can ever be of ufe to reſolve the problem to which the application was intended. In no wife could the piles, drawn out of the Danube, inftruct us better than the fhells that are feen in many of the ftones ufed in building the pyramids of Egypt.

In finifhing this letter, fir, I fhall endeavour to anfwer fome objections made to that part of a work of mine, where I fay,

That there has never been difcovered any monuments of human induſtry, anterior to the deluge.

Some have imagined that I ought to have excluded thofe hatchets of ftone, that have been dug up in Sweden and Germany, from very great depths, and which muft be of great antiquity, having been in ufe before the knowledge of iron and brafs. I al-

low

low that these monuments may be antediluvian; but they may be also very much posterior to this event; for the savages of the new world use them at this day. When, therefore, if such instruments should be found a thousand years hence in Canada, or in the woods of Guiana, whoever should take them for antiquities anterior to the deluge, would entertain an erroneous opinion.

I have seen three sorts of stone hatchets discovered in Germany, and by comparing them with those sent from America, I cannot observe the least difference, either as to form or matter, except that in some of those sent from the new world, there have been found some of the pure agate; which sort of stone has never been discovered amongst those hatchets dug up in Europe, as they say, from great depths. But they are also found in some Celtic tombs,* and upon the superficies of the soil: it happened to me some years ago, to find a hatchet and a hammer of stone, not above half a foot in the ground, in a marshy soil, where I was herbalizing.

* If hatchets of stone are found in the tombs of the ancient Celtes and Germans, they ought to be no longer thought antediluvian.

The

The pyrites ceraunias,† and other stones of hard substances, sometimes argillaceous, sometimes figillaceous, have most commonly been employed by the savages of both continents, before the invention of iron and brass, to make the heads of their arrows, knives, wedges, hatchets, and hammers. Nothing can be more ridiculous, than to hear men, who stile themselves natural philosophers, say, that these instruments are no more than stones naturally so formed, and never destined to the uses attributed to them: but a man can be but little versed in the knowledge of fossils and minerals, not to discover, at first sight, that the stones formed by the *lusus naturae*, are very different from those cut by human art. These naturalists deserve to be sent to the savages of America, who would soon teach them to sharpen a pyrite, and put a handle into it for a hatchet: where they have the double misfortune, to abound in Gold, and to want iron.

Such, sir, are the observations I take the liberty of communicating to you. I could here have added some long remarks, upon the

† Thunderbolt stones.

opinions of thofe who pretend that America has been formerly joined to Africa; but I am unwilling to make fuch an abufe of your time and patience.

The remarkable diftinction between the animals of both continents, and above all between thofe who inhabit the tropics, are conviction enough againft the probability of this hypothefis; of which a more ample difcuffion would retard the pleafure I have in affuring you of the gratitude and refpect with which

I have the honour to be,

Sir,

Your very humble, &c. &c.

3d *November*, 1768.

THE END OF VOL. FIRST.

www.ingramcontent.com/pod-product-compliance
Lightning Source LLC
Chambersburg PA
CBHW030547300426
44111CB00009B/892